Ocean City

Ocean City

by
Kim Kash

TOURIST TOWN GUIDES™

Ocean City (*Tourist Town Guides*™ series)
© 2009 by Kim Kash

Published by:
Channel Lake, Inc., P.O. Box 1771, New York, NY 10156-1771
http://www.channellake.com

Author: Kim Kash
Editors: Elisa Lee, Dirk Vanderwilt
Cover Design: Julianna Lee
Cover Photos: Rick Maloof (rickmaloof.com), iStockphoto

Published in April, 2009

ISBN-13: 978-0-9767064-6-5

For more information, visit http://www.touristtown.com

Help Our Environment!

Even when on vacation, your responsibility to protect the environment does not end. Here are some ways you can help our planet without spoiling your fun:

- ✓ Ask your hotel staff not to clean your towels and bed linens each day. This reduces water waste and detergent pollution.

- ✓ Turn off the lights, heater, and/or air conditioner when you leave your hotel room.

- ✓ Use public transportation when available. Tourist trolleys are very popular, and they are usually cheaper and easier than a car.

- ✓ Recycle everything you can, and properly dispose of rubbish in labeled receptacles.

Tourist towns consume a lot of energy. Have fun, but don't be wasteful. Please do your part to ensure that these attractions are around for future generations to visit and enjoy.

Thank you to Angela Reynolds of Fager's Island, Glenn Irwin of the Ocean City Development Corporation, Mike Cleary of Ocean City Golf Getaway, Susan Jones of the Ocean City Hotel/Motel Association, Donna Abbott with the Town of Ocean City, Eddie Branson at the Gateway Grand, Robert Stevens at the Ocean City Lifesaving Museum, Brian and Kate Mongelli, and the many friends who enthusiastically shared their Ocean City memories and opinions.

A big thanks to my family and friends who supported me in this project by playing mini-golf, eating seafood dinners, shopping, and pub-crawling with me. It was a rough job, and you were there for me.

Mostly, though, I want to thank my husband, Michael Cooney, whose love and unwavering support allowed me to take on this project.

COVER PHOTOS

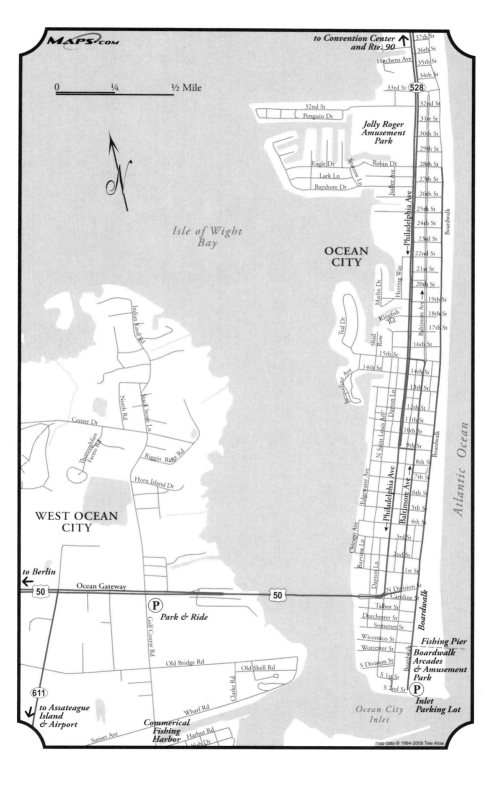

Table of Contents

Introduction

In the late 1800s, Ocean City was conceived and built as a tourist destination; the end of a long journey across hours and miles of flat, empty land; a place to escape from real life and celebrate the summer. It didn't evolve from earlier settlement, and has no roots as a city of trade or industry. Its purpose is to delight vacationers.

Over a hundred years later, that principle is still what gives Ocean City its magic. The trains are gone now; most people visit for a week now rather than for a month or a summer; and off-season activities extend Ocean City's draw more into the cooler months. However, this jumble of buildings, noise, and lights perched at the edge of the sea still stirs up that giddy feeling of summer vacation happiness.

More than eight million people visit Ocean City each year – as many as three million in the "off season." Some try to compare the merits of Ocean City with the smaller, more exclusive Delaware beaches, but that exercise is like comparing apples to oranges, or perhaps surfboards to margaritas. The size and incredible density of Ocean City, coupled with its cheerfully democratic appeal to people of all ages and walks of life, is completely unique.

Ocean City's Boardwalk on a July evening is a study in contrasts. Families, hordes of teenagers, aging bikers, grandparents, blue-collar couples, and folks who just moored their pleasure boats in the commercial harbor all wander up and down the boards. Every possible demographic is here, eating Thrasher's Fries, listening to guitar-strumming buskers, taking a spin on the giant Ferris Wheel, and playing Skee-Ball in the same arcade and perhaps at the very same machine where their parents whiled away a summer evening, decades ago.

Across in West Ocean City, the newer development at the commercial fishing pier sets a newer, more moneyed tone. High-end restaurants, million-dollar condos, and national chains are

muscling their way into what was once a town of local family ven-
tures. Some worry that Ocean City is getting too upscale and its
funky, salt-of-the-earth flavor is fading.

Yet it's hard to cultivate much pretentiousness in Ocean City.
"Exclusive" multi-million-dollar houses have sprung up in a field
behind a popular dinosaur-themed mini-golf park. A high-end day
spa shares a parking lot with a Hooters Restaurant. The Hilton is
right next door to the Thunderbird Motel. And most of Ocean
City's finest restaurants are located in strip malls. The contrasts
between the sublime and the ridiculous are everywhere and this is
precisely what gives Ocean City its enduring, irresistible charm.

Families come back every summer, year after year, and generation after generation because Ocean City is not like real life. It aims
to make people happy.

How to Use this Book

Attractions and vendors listed in this book may have an address,
website (⌂), and/or telephone number (☎). Some items have
other items within them (for example, a restaurant within a hotel).
Sometimes the contact information may be with the inline text, or
there may be no contact information. If there is no contact information, please see the attraction or section heading.

Must-See Attractions: Headlining must-see attractions, or those
that are otherwise iconic or defining, are designated with the 🔲
symbol. The author and/or editor made these and all other qualita-
tive value judgments.

Coverage: This book is not all-inclusive. It is comprehensive,
with many different options for entertainment, dining, eating,
shopping, etc., but there are many establishments not listed here.
Since this is an independent guide, the decision of what to include
was made entirely by the author and/or editor.

Attraction Pricing: When applicable, at the end of each attraction listing is a general pricing reference, indicated by dollar signs, relative to other attractions in the region. The scale is from "$" (least expensive) to "$$$" (most expensive). Contact the attraction directly for specific pricing information. **Please note that** if the attraction is free, or if no pricing information is available at the time of publication, or if a price indication is otherwise irrelevant, then the dollar sign scale is omitted from the listing.

"Family Friendly" Designations: This book mentions attractions that may have a "family friendly" attitude. *However,* this does *not* guarantee that the attraction meets any kind of standards for you or your family. It is merely an opinion that the attraction is generally appropriate for children. You are urged to contact all establishments directly for further information.

History

At the end of the last ice age, the ocean lapped the coast of Maryland 100 miles east of where it does today. The series of barrier islands that frame the mid-Atlantic seaboard were created, and they still continue to shift today as sea levels rise and currents push sand west towards the mainland. To hold back this progression, sand is pumped onto the beaches from offshore every year. The Atlantic's mighty pounding on the shore during a winter storm is a reminder, though, that the balance on this island between human ingenuity and the sheer strength of nature is tenuous. Like its geography, Ocean City's history has been shaped by wind and weather.

THE PLACE ACROSS
The first visitors to this windswept place were the Nanticokes. They didn't live on the island, but crossed the bay from the mainland to hunt and fish there. They named it Assateague, or "the place across."

The first European explorer to come ashore at Assateague may have been Giovanni da Verrazano, who sailed along the coast under a French flag in 1524. His account seems to indicate that he entered what is now Chincoteague Bay and explored inland, calling the area "Arcadia." Some historians dispute this account, declaring that Verrazano's Arcadia was in fact at Kitty Hawk, North Carolina. Nevertheless, in 1976, the bridge that now connects Assateague Island with the mainland was named the Giovanni da Verrazano Bridge in his honor.

In January 1650, over 100 years after Verrazano's voyage, English colonist Henry Norwood and his party were put ashore after their Virginia-bound ship was damaged in a storm. They had been sent to find fresh water and a safe harbor. They were eventually able to reach their Virginia colony after severe hardship, with the assistance of friendly Native Americans. Other than these isolated incidents, the Assateague area was largely unsettled until the mid-1700s, by which time Europeans had pushed most Native Americans from the Eastern Shore. Assateague then served as a spring grazing ground for livestock, which were ferried across from the mainland.

"LADIES RESORT TO THE OCEAN"

In 1868 a group of investors from the Eastern Shore, Baltimore, and Philadelphia formed the Atlantic Hotel Company Corporation to develop an ocean resort on the barrier island. They optioned fifty acres from Stephen Taber, a Long Island businessman who held a patent for an extensive tract on Assateague. The holding that was of interest to the Atlantic Hotel Company Corporation was named "Ladies Resort to the Ocean." Rejecting this fanciful title for their new beach resort, the investors considered Beach City or Sinepuxent City before choosing Ocean City.

The opening of the Atlantic Hotel on July 4, 1875, is generally considered to be the founding date of Ocean City. On that day, at least 800 people boated across the bay for the celebration. Other hotels soon followed, including the Seaside and Congress, as well as a scattering of cottages and fishing camps. The Plimhimmon Hotel opened in 1893. Unlike almost of all the others, this hotel still exists, though it burned down and was rebuilt in the 1960s to look as much as possible like the original. It is now called Plim Plaza.

EARLY RAIL TRAVEL

Travel to Ocean City in its early days meant a ferry ride across the Chesapeake Bay at the crack of dawn, followed by a train ride across the Eastern Shore, and finally a trip in a flat-bottomed scow across the Sinepuxent Bay. Several companies owned the various Eastern Shore railways in the early part of the 20th century, including the Baltimore, Chesapeake, and Atlantic Railway, which soon earned the nickname "Black Cinders and Ashes." Porters, waiting at the station under signs announcing the names of the major hotels, received guests' steamer trunks and parcels and transported them by cart. Meanwhile, the dirty and exhausted travelers walked to their lodgings.

Roads were basically sand trails covered in crushed oyster shells and cars could only access the island by rattling across the train bridge.

THE LIFE SAVING SERVICE

In 1878, Captain William T. West and six other men manned Ocean City's first lifesaving station on the northernmost point of town at Caroline Street and the Boardwalk. In 1915, the Life Saving Service merged with the Revenue Cutter Service to form the U.S. Coast Guard, and Ocean City became one of the few beach resorts to have a lifeboat station. Until 1930, when the Ocean City Beach Patrol was formed, the Coast Guard responded to swimmers as well as boaters in distress. The Coast Guard still has a station in Ocean City, now located on the bayside at the south end of Philadelphia Avenue. The Ocean City Museum Society moved the old station building to the southern end of the Boardwalk in 1977, where it now houses the Ocean City Life-Saving Station Museum.

TRIMPER'S WINDSOR RESORT

The Sinepuxent Beach Company of Baltimore City bought more of Stephen Taber's land both north and south of the original resort in 1890, and sold 25-by-142-foot lots, starting at $25. The city was incorporated in 1894, and a mayor was elected from the Sinepuxent Beach Company board.

In 1892, Daniel Trimper and his wife purchased a number of these lots and established The Windsor Resort Amusement Center, creating two blocks of rides, vaudeville shows, games, and other attractions that still form the nucleus of today's brightly lit Boardwalk hustle and bustle. There was no electricity on the island yet, and Trimper at one point hooked a generator to two steam engines to power the rides and lights. They bought one of the finest carousels in America in 1902 and installed it in Ocean City. The carousel's grand parade of horses, ostriches, lions, and other gorgeous, fanciful animals still circles round and round today in an indoor portion of the Boardwalk arcade. The carousel was painstakingly restored in the 1980s by Daniel's grandson, Granville.

THE BOARDWALK AND PIER

The earliest version of the Boardwalk was "built" in 1902 when wood planks were laid directly in the sand along two blocks. Each day before high tide, they were taken up and stored on the porches of the big hotels. Later, even after sections were more firmly anchored in the sand, they were still removed and stored during the winter. The first permanent Boardwalk was built in 1910, and extended for five blocks north from the southern end of town. In 1912, the Boardwalk was raised ten to twelve feet above the sand, and remained elevated until the early 1940s.

The pier and its buildings were built in 1907. Over the years, they have been wrecked by storm, fire, and ice, and rebuilt, restored, and repurposed. Inside the original pier building was a dance pavilion, plus bowling alleys, a billiards room, and a silent-movie theater. A fishing pier extended from the main building out into the ocean, and was capped at its end by a second building, which was a roller-skating rink.

During what many consider to be Ocean City's cultural heyday, the pier's ballroom swayed to the sounds of performances by the Glenn Miller Orchestra, Jimmy Dorsey, and Benny Goodman. Vacationers dressed in their finest attire when attending such events, and were expected to dress formally every day for lunch and dinner as well.

THE GREAT FIRE OF 1925

Ocean City was wired for electricity soon after turn of the 20th century. In December 1925 a catastrophic fire began in the town's electric plant, destroying the Atlantic Hotel as well as another hotel, the pier and its buildings, and three blocks of downtown. Of all the hotels lost, only the Atlantic was rebuilt.

THE GREAT STORM OF 1933

In what turned out to be one of Ocean City's luckiest natural disasters, a huge storm in 1933 slashed an inlet right through the barrier island, creating a channel from Sinepuxent Bay to the ocean. This created Maryland's only ocean harbor and the beginning of blue-water fishing out of Ocean City. White Marlin fishing began shortly thereafter, and the Ocean City Marlin Club was founded in 1936.

Much of the Boardwalk was washed away by this same storm, and after that the U.S. Army Corps of Engineers extended long rock jetties out into the water north and south of the newly-formed inlet. This caused large amounts of sand to be deposited on the beach just north of the inlet by the action of the wind and waves that grew wider and wider in the 1940s. It was then that local officials decided to lower the Boardwalk to the level of the sand. Older hotels built stairways down to it, while newer hotels were constructed at the new, lower level.

THE AUTO ERA

The 1933 storm that created the inlet also badly damaged the railroad bridges over the Choptank and Nanticoke Rivers and the Sinepuxent Bay. By then the roads were much improved and the decision was made to repair an auto bridge, but not the railroad bridges. This marked the end of the era of train travel across the Eastern Shore and the dawn of a whole new car culture in Ocean City. Hearing the roar of traffic now on Coastal Highway, it's hard to imagine the city without them.

In the summer of 1939, Ocean Highway (today's Coastal Highway) opened to serve the increasing auto traffic, connecting Ocean City and the Delaware beaches. By around 1950, motels were opening up north of 29th Street (which had been the city line for a time) and soon the city annexed everything up to 146th St., which is the Delaware border.

With Ocean City growing as an important Maryland tourist destination, Governor William Preston Lane made the decision to build a bridge across the Chesapeake Bay. A 1938 study had demonstrated an economic necessity for it, but construction wasn't started until 1949. The bridge was initially nicknamed Lane's Folly because many thought the governor was crazy for undertaking such a huge, expensive project. At the time, it was the world's longest over-water steel structure. The bridge opened July 30, 1952, ending ferry service across the Chesapeake Bay. The second span opened in June of 1973. Ocean City experienced dramatic growth following the opening of the bay bridge.

OCEAN CITY GROWS UP

In July of 1962, Bobby Baker's Carousel Hotel opened in North Ocean City, ushering in a new era of high-rolling sophistication, along with a large dose of controversy and scandal. Limousines and champagne-stocked motor coaches brought big-name Washington guests to the hotel's opening, including Vice President Lyndon Johnson and Lady Bird Johnson. The Carousel had a heated pool, two cocktail lounges with black-clad hostesses, and large, elegantly appointed suites. The Carousel's aura of moneyed elegance paved the way for the city's uptown district of luxury high-rise hotels and condominiums, so different in look and feel from the old downtown district.

Baker was a key figure in Washington politics, but he was forced to resign his government position amidst accusations of fraud and income tax evasion. He ultimately spent several months in federal prison. Even after his hotel was sold, many still called it Bobby Baker's Carousel. And for many in Ocean City he personifies that glamorous – and troubled – era.

In 1970, Ocean City's first high-rise condo was built: the 14-story High Point at 114th Street. A condominium construction boom followed on the oceanfront in North Ocean City. But by 1975 the market went bust and almost every building went into foreclosure, with thousands of condos sitting empty. In a few years, however, the market caught up and the building began again. This cycle of building and market glut has continued to some degree ever since.

ENVIRONMENT VS. PROPERTY RIGHTS

In another chapter of Ocean City's history written by wind and water, a huge storm in 1962 flattened the beach's protective dunes and waves crashed all the way across the island to meet the swelling bayside waters. When the storm was over, some parts of the beaches had been narrowed over 100 feet. In some cases, not just summer cottages were washed away, but the entire plots on which they sat. The Worcester County shore was declared a national disaster area.

This storm brought to the public's attention the necessity for environmental regulation to supersede the rights of individual property owners. Over the next several years, a continuous string of dunes and walls were built. In some cases, private land had to be ceded to the city in order for this construction to take place. It was clear that these measures were necessary in order to safeguard the billions of dollars of property that sat so close to the ocean on this fragile land.

In the early 1970s, the city also began bulldozing the beach to push sand back up on the ever-eroding shore. Today the beach is replenished by pumping sand in from offshore. Miami Beach maintains its shoreline in the same manner.

During this same period, there was a growing awareness of the importance of wetlands to water quality and the health of fish populations among other environmental and economic concerns. Prior to this, marshy areas were seen as having little or no value, and large building projects in the late 1960s were systematically dredging and filling the bayside of North Ocean City. In 1970, the

Maryland Wetlands Act established a legal definition of "wetlands" and a permitting process for anything that would alter them. A series of major developments planned for the bayside of West Ocean City were scuttled shortly thereafter.

RESTORING "OLD O.C."

In recent decades, the year-round population of Ocean City has grown, and new city public works projects, parks and amenities are serving a larger, permanent population as well as ever-growing crowds of summer tourists.

New building density regulations were written in the 1980s as permanent residents became increasingly vocal about unrestrained development in Ocean City. However, that was like closing the barn door after the horse had bolted. Thus, a movement began around that time to "save" the old downtown Ocean City – this time not from fire or flood, but from rampant modernization.

To that end, in 2000 the Ocean City Development Corporation was founded. This non-profit organization created a set of architectural design standards for the oldest sections of town to encourage new building projects to incorporate design elements from Ocean City's early days. They have installed educational plaques on the 20 oldest buildings. They also have given grants to property owners for façade improvements, and these are starting to give the old downtown a charming turn-of-the-century patina. It's hard, though, to imagine what a vacationer dressed and ready for an evening on the Boardwalk circa 1900 would have thought of today's tourist wearing nothing but a bathing suit, a rude t-shirt and a smile.

Area Orientation

Ocean City is Maryland's only ocean beach and harbor. Ocean City stretches ten miles from the inlet at its southern end to the Delaware state line. In some places the island is only two or three blocks wide. Aerial photographs show that Ocean City is a delicate, thin spit of an island, and in fact, several storms have nearly flattened it.

To get a sense of Ocean City's ephemeral geological status, it's interesting to stand at the inlet and look south, across the open channel of water connecting the inland bay with the Atlantic Ocean. This inlet was gouged out during a 1933 storm. Before this storm Ocean City and Assateague were joined as a single island. Now, rock jetties, which keep the channel open, reinforce the inlet and Ocean City's beaches are replenished every winter by pumping in offshore sand. Therefore, the physical configuration of the island remains more or less constant, thanks to sheer human determination. Assateague, on the other hand, has been left to weather naturally, and the whole island is marching rapidly westward. So, fifty years, ago the island of Assateague was directly across the channel; now it sits about a half mile to the west.

Ocean City's bustling streets and bright skyline have an almost fairytale quality when first glimpsed from the west. Maybe that's because it takes at least three hours to get to Ocean City by car from the nearest major cities, and passengers are thrilled that the trip is almost over. Maybe it's because Ocean City's tall buildings and bright lights rise up suddenly at the edge of flat, quiet Eastern Shore farmland. Either way, there's no denying the little thrill at that first glimpse of Ocean City from either the Route 50 or the Route 90 bridge.

A VACATION FOR EVERYONE

Ocean City spends many advertising dollars touting itself as a family-friendly destination. With its waterparks, mini-golf courses, and beautiful beaches, it is wonderful for families with small children. Ocean City also has over 250 bars within its city limits, making it the ideal place for an outrageously lubricated vacation for adults. The contrast is sometimes striking, especially on the Boardwalk, where families with small children stroll elbow-to-elbow with beery pub-crawlers. This is part of Ocean City's charm, actually. Everyone belongs, and everyone is happy to be on vacation.

GETTING TO OCEAN CITY

Unlike the early days of Ocean City, when vacationers would spend a very long day on the train and arrive at the beach exhausted and grimy with coal dust, there is no longer any train service to Ocean City. You can get to Ocean City via **Greyhound Bus** *(200 North Philadelphia Ave.* ☎ *800.231.2222* ⁂ *greyhound.com)*. However, most people drive to Ocean City.

Travelers from Washington and Baltimore must take Route 50 and cross the Chesapeake Bay Bridge, which is beautiful but can cause enormous, legendary traffic jams. During the summer season, it is madness to try to drive to Ocean City on a Friday evening, or return to the western shore on a Sunday afternoon. Plan your vacation so that you are not on the road during these peak traffic times. The **Maryland Transportation Authority** *(*☎ *877.BAYSPAN* ⁂ *baybridge.com)* has current bridge traffic conditions. Call or visit their website before you travel to get the latest on traffic. These sources will also alert you to any bridge maintenance currently underway. Bridge repairs are frequent and can cause severe traffic backups.

Once across the bridge, Route 50 continues all the way into Ocean City. Route 50 is also known as Ocean Gateway on the Eastern Shore. Alternatively, vacationers wishing to enter Ocean

City further north can take the exit off of Route 50 for Route 90 about twelve miles west of Ocean City, and follow that road into town instead. Route 90 ends in Ocean City at 62nd Street.

Travelers coming from New York and other northern points will take 95 South to Route 1, then follow Routes 1 and 113 south to Route 50, just west of Ocean City. This route covers the whole length of Delaware on the east side of the Chesapeake Bay, and thus avoids the Bay Bridge.

GETTING AROUND

Finding your way around Ocean City is easy since in many places it is only two or three blocks wide! Coastal Highway is the big north-south road through town. In the southern part of town, it splits into two streets: Baltimore Avenue on the ocean side and Philadelphia Avenue on the bayside.

At the southern, or inlet, part of town, the east-west streets are named after Maryland counties. Then the numbered streets start, and they run from 1st Street all the way up to 146th Street at the Delaware state line. A few named streets are thrown in between the numbered streets, but for the most part, the streets march northward in an orderly, ascending numerical fashion.

Street numbers are intuitive: the Convention Center, for example, is at 4001 Coastal Highway, or at 40th Street and Coastal Highway. Often places are identified as being either ocean side or bayside, which makes it even easier to navigate.

During the summer season, parking is a challenge – and one that can and should be avoided. If you're a glutton for punishment, though, you can drive around and look for parking. Much of the downtown street parking has the modern equivalent of a meter; look for the machine on the sidewalk within a half block or so of your car and buy a ticket for however long you want to stay, then put the ticket on your dashboard. Or, you can park at the inlet lot

for $2 per hour during peak season. Lines can develop getting in
and out of this lot.

LOCAL BUS SERVICE

Ocean City has bus service that runs up and down Coastal Highway 24 hours a day, 7 days a week, from the inlet to the Delaware
line. The bus costs just $2 for an all-day pass that lasts from 6 a.m.
to 6 a.m. the following day. Sometimes it's noisy and crowded, but
riding the bus can actually be a lot of fun. Riders are often chatty
and high-spirited, and conversations spring up between unlikely
groups (middle-aged couples returning from dinner and teenagers
heading out to play a night round of mini-golf, for example.) From
April through October, there is also service to a park-and-ride lot
in West Ocean City. Complete schedule information is available
online (⌖ ococean.com/busflyer.html).

TAXI SERVICE

Ocean City taxis charge a $3 initial fare and about $2 per mile, with
possible add-on charges.

Ocean City is a favorite destination for classic car enthusiasts
during several classic car weekends throughout the year. You can
call **Classic Taxi** (☎ 410.289.1960 ⌖ classictaxi.org) any time,
though, for a ride in such classics as a '66 Chrysler Newport, a '64
Galaxie, or a '61 Cadillac Fleetwood painted pink and white.

If you'd prefer a more modern cab ride, there are several taxi
services in Ocean City. A few mainstays are **A Beach Taxi** (☎
410.524.TAXI/410.289.TAXI ⌖ oceancitymdtaxi.com), **Dave's Taxi**
(☎ 410.250.2400) and **Sunshine Cab** (☎ 410.208.2828).

WALKING

Walking is highly recommended whenever possible in Ocean City.
There are crosswalks at about every intersection. Families cross
Coastal Highway by the hundreds every morning like migrating sea

turtles, heading east towards the ocean carrying coolers, beach chairs, umbrellas, blankets, and sand toys.

Coastal Highway is lined on either side with sidewalks, but it can be a noisy and unpleasant walk. Try heading a half block away from it, either on the bayside or ocean side, and you may find walkways or alleyways that parallel Coastal Highway. These smaller routes are a bit more peaceful, and walking through the side streets and alleys is a nice way to check out the neighborhoods that are tucked away behind the buildings fronting Coastal Highway.

Of course, the most beautiful walk is along the beach itself. All of Ocean City's beaches are public, so feel free to wander up and down the seashore as far as you want. There are dune crossings at every block, and at a midpoint between each block.

There is no continuous public bayside access, so walking along the shore of the bay is not an option.

BEACH ACCESS FOR PEOPLE WITH DISABILITIES

People who use wheelchairs will want to check out the **Beach Wheelchair Program** (☎ *410.723.6610* ⏍ *ococean.com/beachch.html*) run by the Town of Ocean City. Beach wheelchairs are provided by the beach patrol at fifteen locations on a first-come, first-served basis, from Memorial Day to Labor Day. Also, there are twenty dune crossings that are designed to provide easier access for people with physical challenges.

DOGS

Dogs are not allowed on the beach at all from May 1 to September 30. So in the cooler seasons, Ocean City is a suitable place for a doggie vacation, but please leave pets at home when you vacation there during the summer months. Ocean City has a **Dog Playground** at 94th Street (*⏍ ococean.com/dogplayground.html*), but you must register and pay a fee to use it. This is the only place in Ocean City where off-leash dogs are permitted.

LOCAL SERVICES

Ocean City has many services you might need away from home. Much of the town is shuttered during the winter, but even then, there are choices for banking, shopping, health care, and the like.

There is a complete list of Ocean City ordinances on their website (🖰 *ococean.com/ord.html*) covering dog restrictions, sleeping on the beach, drinking in public, biking on the Boardwalk, and various other things that might trip you up.

HOSPITALS AND CLINICS

Atlantic General Hospital *(9733 Healthway Dr.* 🖰 *atlanticgeneral.org)* is the closest hospital, with an emergency room and all the services of a regional hospital. Atlantic General also runs **Atlantic ImmediCare**, *(1001 Philadelphia Ave.* ☎ *410.289.0065* 🖰 *atlanticimmedicare.com)* a walk-in daytime primary care facility open during the spring and summer. Atlantic ImmediCare treats accidents, injuries and unexpected illnesses, and they offer vaccinations, blood pressure screening, occupational medicine, and sports injury treatment.

There are a few other clinics on the island as well. **75th Street Medical Center** *(7408 Coastal Hwy* ☎ *410.524.0075* 🖰 *75thstmedical.com)* and **126th Street Medical Center** *(12601-D Coastal Hwy* ☎ *410.250.8000* 🖰 *75thstmedical.com)* are open all year, with expanded summer hours. They do not bill insurance companies, but will take postdated checks.

Your Doc's In *(103 120th St* ☎ *410.520.0582* 🖰 *yourdocsin.com)* is another urgent care center with hours that vary depending on the season. Your Doc's In accepts most insurances.

POST OFFICE

Ocean City has two post office locations: **408 Philadelphia Avenue** (☎ *410.289.7819)* and **7101 Coastal Highway** *(☎ 410.524.7611).*

BANKING

Many national and regional banks have branch offices in Ocean City, and ATMs are plentiful around town. **Western Union** has locations at **7-Eleven** *(5809 Coastal Hwy ☎ 410.723.1442)*, and at **E Point Internet Café** *(1513 Philadelphia Ave. ☎ 410.289.9844)*, and others in West Ocean City.

RESTROOMS

Ocean City maintains eight public restroom facilities along the Boardwalk and at the public transit stations. The facilities are large and basically clean, considering the enormous volume of traffic moving through them. There are rinse-off showers available at three locations: Caroline Street, Inlet Beach, and 9th Street.

LOCAL PUBLICATIONS

The **Maryland Coast Dispatch** *(🖰 mdcoastdispatch.com)* is Ocean City's newspaper, and it is published weekly. **Beachcomber** is Ocean City's entertainment weekly, with dining and entertainment reviews, and an events calendar. Tourists may also want to pick up the free *Ocean City Visitors Guide.* The editorial content is pure marketing patter, but the magazine is stuffed with coupons, and has a useful advertiser index.

LIBRARY

Ocean City has a large, beautiful new **Public Library** *(10003 Coastal Hwy ☎ 410.524.1818 🖰 worcesterlibrary.org)*. The airy, two-story building is stocked with great beach reads, of course. Even in non-fiction, it would stand up nicely in comparison with any suburban public library's collection. Anyone can apply for a library card and check out materials. The library has computers available for patrons' use, free wireless Internet, and a room full of materials about Ocean City's history.

PLACES OF WORSHIP

Ocean City has about a dozen **churches** (⁀ð *ocean-city.com/local/churches.shtml*), with many others in the surrounding communities of Berlin, Ocean Pines, and Bishopville. **St. Paul's By the Sea Episcopal Church** is of historical significance, as it has been standing at the corner of Baltimore Avenue and 3rd Streets since the turn of the 20th century. The church has a labyrinth on the floor of its fellowship hall. On Wednesday nights from 7 p.m. to 9 p.m. in the summer, they offer a candlelit labyrinth walk, which is a meditative practice shared by many spiritual traditions.

FOR MORE INFORMATION...

The **Ocean City Chamber of Commerce** (*12320 Ocean Gateway* ☎ *410.213.0552* ⁀ð *oceancity.org*) is an easy stop on the way into Ocean City, and is open every day from 9 a.m. to 5 p.m. The staff is friendly and knowledgeable about all things Ocean City, and the lobby is stocked with flyers and brochures for dining, attractions, and lodging, plus all the local newspapers and coupon circulars.

Inside the Roland E. Powell Convention Center on Coastal Highway at 40th Street is the **Ocean City Visitors Bureau**. Much of the same information is available here as at the Chamber of Commerce, and staff can also help if you'd like to plan a big family or corporate event in town.

SEASONS AND TEMPERATURES

Ocean City's temperatures are fair most of the year, with summer Fahrenheit temperatures usually in the 80s and winter lows averaging in the high 20s or low 30s. Usually in the summertime, ocean breezes make even the hottest, most humid days feel comfortable – but still days can be quite sticky.

The ideal time to visit Ocean City is September and October, when the summer crowds are gone but almost all the businesses are still open. The weather is still balmy, and the ocean temperatures are at their warmest. Many refer to this time of year as the "second season." The weather remains temperate through November, though every week it gets a little cooler, and a few more shops and restaurants close up for the winter.

From December through mid-March, the cold, wet air seeps into the bones. Winter walks on the beach can be exhilarating, but it's important to dress for warmth and protection against the wind, because 30 degrees on the beach feels much more extreme than 30 degrees just a mile inland. The winter cold can make an off-season beach stay really cozy, though, if you choose accommodations that have a fireplace or a snug, warm spot from which to view the elements outside.

Springtime in Ocean City has its own charm. Shopkeepers and homeowners are repainting and repairing after a winter of salt air and winds, and preparing for the coming season. Ocean City is noisy this time of year with construction sounds, as construction and renovation picks up when the temperatures rise. Spring tends to be a wet season; the rain and the warmer temperatures seem to sharpen the briny scent in the air.

FESTIVALS AND EVENTS

The Town of Ocean City puts on festivals, conventions, and city-wide events almost every weekend of the year *(⌐ oco-cean.com/calframe.html)*. Whether you're a car enthusiast, a sandcastle builder, or an arts and crafts fan, you can plan your vacation around an event that ties in with your interests. Check the website for specific dates.

SPRINGFEST
(May) This four-day outdoor party happens every May. Crafters and food vendors set up stalls in big-top tents at the inlet parking lot. An outdoor stage offers regional and national musical acts. Performers have included The Fabulous Hubcaps and Randy Travis.

MARYLAND STATE FIREMAN'S ASSOCIATION CONFERENCE AND PARADE
(June ⌐ msfa.org/content/conventioninfo) Many professional associations hold annual events in Ocean City, but none do it with the same gusto as the Fireman's Association. Held every June, this weeklong event includes exhibits open to the public at the convention center, dinners and celebrations at bars and restaurants all over town. A three-hour parade marches down Coastal Highway on Wednesday afternoon and Ocean City is flooded with fire and rescue vehicles both new and antique, and thousands of partying firefighters from all over the state.

INDEPENDENCE DAY
(July) Ocean City puts on not one, but two big July 4th parties. One celebration happens on the beach at North Division Street with a concert and fireworks. The other is bayside at Northside Park, with games, entertainment, food, and fireworks.

DELMARVA BIKE WEEK

(September ⌁ delmarvabikeweek.com) Over 100,000 motorcycling enthusiasts travel to Ocean City and Berlin in early September for Delmarva Bike Week. Bikers cruise up and down Coastal Highway enjoying parties at bars, restaurants and clubs all over town, plus mechanical bull riding contests, tattoo contests, poolside bikini contests, pudding wrestling contests (seriously!) and plenty of live music. The noise is deafening all weekend; the sight of parking lots absolutely full of nothing but motorcycles, some of them tricked out with colored lights, is incredible.

SUNFEST

(September) Kicking off Ocean City's "second season" in September, Sunfest is the town's biggest festival of the year. The inlet parking lot is set up with two stages of live entertainment, and tents with food and arts and crafts vendors. The festival includes such fall-themed children's activities as scarecrow making and pumpkin decorating. Meanwhile, the Sunfest Kite Festival happens between North Division Street and 5th Street, with children's workshops, kite battles, and a sport kite competition.

CAR SHOWS

Car enthusiasts will enjoy the **OC Car and Truck Show** *(⌁ occarshow.com)*, the **Mid-Atlantic Classic Chevy Festival** in June, **Endless Summer Cruisin'** hot rods events on Columbus Day weekend, and various other auto-related gatherings throughout the year. If you're a car enthusiast – classic or otherwise – Ocean City is an east coast haven. A local car club, the **Ocean City Cruzers** *(⌁ occruzers.com)* keeps a good list of area automotive events and car clubs.

WINTERFEST

(November - January) At the inlet parking lot, take an extensive tour of holiday lights from the warmth of your own car. Then drive

north along Ocean City's street, lined with lighted wreaths, to Northside Park. At this large bayside park, hundreds of animated lighted displays are set up, which can be toured by tram for a small fee. Winterfest's displays are set up from late November through January 1st.

The Boardwalk

The signature attraction of Ocean City is the Boardwalk. Stretching for three miles from the inlet at its southernmost point up to 28th Street, the Boardwalk is a promenade for socializing, shopping, biking, eating, playing, people-watching, and gazing across the golden sand at the ocean. On summer evenings the Boardwalk is as crowded as a Manhattan sidewalk. Instead of suits, though, people on the Boardwalk are more likely to be wearing their favorite vacation clothing: bathing suits, tiny sundresses, shorts and t-shirts, biker gear, baggy jeans and sneakers, you name it. It's a far cry from the turn of the century, when the Boardwalk was created and vacationers promenaded in their very finest and most formal – and probably really hot – clothing.

Also unlike 1902, when the Boardwalk was a portable affair that was rolled up and stored on hotel porches at high tide, today's Boardwalk is a wide and permanent fixture with a **tram** (*ococean.com/busflyer.html*) running up and down the middle of it.

Seasonal Hours: Many Boardwalk attractions, shops, and restaurants are open only during the main summer tourist season. There may be a few that are open (with limited hours) during the off-season, so contact the establishment directly if you intend on visiting Ocean City during this time.

Important Note: The Boardwalk is also called Atlantic Avenue; some addresses use "Boardwalk" and some "Atlantic Avenue." This book uses "Boardwalk" for consistency.

BOARDWALK ATTRACTIONS

Most of Ocean City's attractions are either on or accessible directly from the Boardwalk. Just by strolling, visitors find a myriad of unique playtime opportunities.

TRIMPER'S RIDES [MUST SEE]

(Boardwalk at the Inlet ☎ 410.289.8617 ⌂ beach-net.com/trimpers/)
Established in 1897, Trimper's rides, games, and attractions have
been the Boardwalk's anchor since the very beginning. The crown
jewel of Trimper's is the restored 1902 carousel, with its vividly
painted, hand-carved horses, lions, exotic birds and other animals
that vacationing children have ridden for over 100 years. The carousel is, understandably, tucked back inside the arcade building,
away from the elements. Walk in through other antique kiddie rides
– and some not as well restored – and check out the carousel
whether or not you have children. Trimper's also has the whole
range of outdoor carnival rides: a small roller coaster, pirate ship,
tilt-a-whirl, teacups, and many others. The Haunted House ride,
with cars in the shape of coffins, is a perennial, if threadbare, favorite. Teens might think its corny, glow-in-the-dark spooks are stu-
pid. However, if you watch for adults emerging from the ride,
you'll see some laughing so hard that tears are streaming down
their faces.

MARTY'S PLAYLAND

(Boardwalk & Worcester St. ☎ 410.289.7271) The Boardwalk arcades
pack in pinball, antique Skee-ball lanes, air hockey, arcades and
miniature crane games. Carnival-style barkers encourage visitors to
try their luck at the pool table and the basketball hoop, at Whack-a-
Mole. The din of noise and lights is intoxicating on a summer
night.

THE PIER

(☎ 410.289.3477 ⌂ jollyrogerpark.com) Jolly Roger operates the rides
and games on Ocean City's pier. Don't miss the giant Ferris wheel,
which offers a spectacular view of the beach, the inlet, and all of
downtown Ocean City. If you prefer to experience similar heights
within a matter of seconds, choose the Slingshot, which catapults
you and a friend straight up in a little round pod that's tethered to

the pier by a couple of industrial-strength bungee cords. Check their web site for information about the Jolly Rogers Passport to Fun for admission to rides here and at their 30th Street park.

RIPLEY'S BELIEVE IT OR NOT

(401 S Atlantic Ave./Pier Building on the Boardwalk ☎ *410.289.5600* ✆ *ripleysoceancity.com)* The giant, animatronic shark bursting through the front and side of the Ripley's Believe It Or Not building is a pretty accurate preview of the kinds of things you will see inside this silly, creepy "odditorium." Robert L. Ripley was a collector of random odd and amazing things from around the world, and the artist who drew the *Ripley's Believe It Or Not* cartoons for the Sunday newspapers for decades. His collection of weird stuff is displayed in museums around the world. Ocean City's location has on display: a pair of traditional Japanese foot-binding shoes, genuine shrunken heads, a Fiji Island cannibal fork, a vampire killing kit from the 1850s containing a cross, a pistol, silver bullets, and holy water, Medieval torture masks, a portrait of Queen Elizabeth the First done in lint, a two-headed calf and a headless chicken. At $12.99 per adult ticket and $7.99 for a child, Ripley's is not cheap. But on a rainy or sweltering hot day, it's a fun way to spend some time.

OCEAN CITY LIFE-SAVING STATION MUSEUM 🏅

(813 South Boardwalk ☎ *410.289.4991* ✆ *ocmuseum.org)* One of the best-preserved life-saving stations still standing, this small but fascinating museum tells the story of how the U.S. Lifesaving Service (which was later folded into the Coast Guard) kept a constant vigil on the Assateague coastline. The whole area was once called Assateague Island until the 1933 storm that created today's inlet dividing the southern end of Ocean City from Assateague. Here is the place to get an excellent, pleasant history lesson about Ocean City – and to take a look at the shockingly small, low-tech lifesaving boats and devices that were used in shipwreck rescues only a hun-

dred years ago. The museum also has an interesting exhibit consisting of small dishes of sand from beaches all over the world. From California to Christmas Island, Tasmania to Japan to Jamaica, the sand displayed shows the surprising variety of colors and textures of sand around the world. It especially shows how pale and smooth Ocean City's sand is compared to other beach resorts. Upstairs, a series of intricate dollhouses depict old Ocean City. Mermaid-themed art fills another room. Early bathing fashions, including scratchy wool suits, are also displayed. Finally, case after case of dishes and other shipwreck artifacts create an eerie reminder of how many vessels wrecked on the shoals off Ocean City in the not-too-distant past. Call or check the web site for the schedule of daily talks on the Boardwalk in front of the museum. Topics include Ocean City history, sharks, knot tying, and other educational and kid-friendly topics.

BIBLICAL SAND SCULPTURES 🅼🆂

(On the beach at 2nd St. ⏚ randyhofman.com) Since 1981, painter and sculptor Randy Hofman has been creating large and vividly detailed sculptures in the sand portraying biblical scenes and stories. Some are fairly simple and take him only a few hours to complete. For a more complicated sculpture – of the Last Supper, for example – Hofman will begin at 10 in the morning, and work straight through until 4 a.m. the next day. He sprays the finished sculpture with a mixture of water and Elmer's Glue to give it staying power, while his tool of choice is a simple plastic crab-picking knife. Often he leaves a plastic jug with religious tracts for people who are interested in learning more. Hofman's sand sculptures are impressive works of art, which, like the Tibetan Buddhist sand mandalas, are all the more beautiful because they are so fragile and temporary.

BOARDWALK SHOPPING

While it may seem that the only thing to buy along the Boardwalk are t-shirts emblazoned with outrageous messages or biker logos, there are several shops that are worth a second look.

OCEAN GALLERY 🏆 MUST SEE!

(Boardwalk & 2nd St. ☎ 410.289.5300) Understatement is not the way they do business at the Ocean Gallery. Joe Kro-Art, who calls himself "the P.T. Barnum of Fine Art," originally opened this over-whelming jumble of a fine art store in order to sell his own photographs and paintings at the beach. The exterior of the building is completely covered in architectural parts of other buildings from all over the world – many of them painted neon orange. Inside, paintings, prints, and posters are piled and hung and stacked every which way in a multi-storied maze of rooms. There is something here for every taste: posters of cute kittens, of Marilyn Monroe, and of girls in bikinis draped over cars, paintings copying the masters, original oils and watercolors of beach scenes, seascapes, still lifes, and landscapes. For all its kitsch, the gallery sells original fine art from some of Maryland's most accomplished artists, focusing on regional themes such as crabs, lighthouses, landscapes, etc. Sprinkled throughout are hilariously cheesy snapshots of a tuxedo-clad Joe Kro-Art and an endless string of celebrity models in bikinis, making special appearances at Ocean Gallery. There are two other locations, but this is the original and best one.

KITE LOFT

(The Boardwalk at 5th St. ☎ 410.289.6852 ⏷ kiteloft.com) A wonder-land of kites, windsocks, banners, whirligigs and yard flags, Kite Loft is the place to go at the start of a family beach vacation to pick up a kite that can be flown at the beach all week. The Kite Loft hosts spectacular kite festivals each spring and fall, and even if

you're not a kite-flyer yourself, watching hundreds of kites flying above the beach is a lot of fun. The Kite Loft has been an Ocean City fixture for over 30 years. There are three Kite Loft stores in town, and the Boardwalk at 5th Street location is its headquarters.

EDWARDS DEPARTMENT STORE

(The Boardwalk at N Division St. ☎ *410.289.7000* ⏚ *ocedwards.com)* Edwards has a more upscale selection of surf clothing, gifts, accessories and sunglasses than other Boardwalk shops. What's great about Edwards, though, is the shoe department called Footloose (it has its own entrance from the Boardwalk). They sell a good selection of Roxy, Sperry, Vans, Minnetonka, and other high-quality, beachy brands. Prices are steep, but that is to be expected considering the location and the brands carried. They have a great sale at the end of the summer season.

MALIBU'S SURF SHOP

(713 Boardwalk ☎ *410.289.3000* ⏚ *malibus.com)* This charming little surf shop is the only one on the Boardwalk, and locals know to call them for accurate surf reports. Located in an old oceanfront house, Malibu's Surf Shop has a large selection of longboards and shortboards, wetsuits and other gear. You can also call Malibu's for surf lessons. They offer private and small group lessons in the mornings and sometimes after 5:30 p.m. during the season. Malibu's provides the surfboards for the lessons, and can teach everyone from 5-year-olds to grandparents!

FLASHBACK OLD-TIME PHOTOS

(The Boardwalk at 1st St. ☎ *410.289.4256/The Boardwalk at Somerset St.* ☎ *410.289.2598* ⏚ *oldtimephotos.com)* No trip to the beach is complete without a sepia-toned family photograph with dad in a waistcoat and top hat, mom with a plumed hat and a shotgun, and grim-faced little ones in stiff Victorian garb. This is a much better beach souvenir than a hermit crab. The 1st Street location is open

daily from March through October, and Saturdays and Sundays from November through February.

TELESCOPE PICTURES

(☎ *410.289.0685* ✇ *ocbeachphotos.com*) Dozens of Telescope Picture photographers train hard each spring, running laps up and down the soft beach sand to prepare for a summer season taking vacation photos from the inlet to the Delaware line. Look for Telescope Picture photographers on the beach seven days a week from May through September. High school students and family groups alike can pose on the sand or in the surf for group photos that are sealed into little plastic "telescopes" to create a 3-D effect. You can also order a variety of other items with your photos emblazoned on them such as mouse pads, ornaments, coffee mugs, etc.

SNACKS ON THE BOARDWALK

Many Ocean City memories revolve around particular snack foods that have been made right on the Boardwalk by locally owned businesses for decades. Snacking on the Boardwalk is a favorite tradition.

THRASHER'S FRENCH FRIES

(*801 Boardwalk* ☎ *410.289.4150*) Thrasher's has been making fries on the Boardwalk since 1929, and they've got it down to a science. They don't make anything but fries, and they don't offer any choice about condiments beyond salt and apple cider vinegar. Ketchup? Not an option. They use peanut oil for frying because it's (relatively) healthy and gives the fries a nice, light crunch. To sit on a bench on the Boardwalk and share a big bucket of salty, vinegary Thrasher's fries with a friend is one of the finest Ocean City pleasures.

FISHER'S POPCORN

(Boardwalk at Talbot St. ☎ *410.289.5638* ✆ *fisherspopcorn.com)* Fisher's makes buttered, caramel, and cheese popcorn, and has been popping corn on the Boardwalk since 1937. You can get some to eat as you stroll the Boardwalk, and you can also order tins of popcorn to be mailed as gifts.

DUMSER'S DAIRYLAND

(601 South Boardwalk/14 South Boardwalk/5 Wicomico St. ☎ *410.289.0934* ✆ *beach-net.com/dumsers)* Dumser's has two full-service restaurants on Coastal Highway, and one on Philadelphia Avenue just a block off the Boardwalk. On the Boardwalk, though, their three stands stick to the basics with a big assortment of ice cream flavors and toppings, and soft serve ice cream available by the cup or the cone. Dumser's has been an Ocean City fixture since 1939. The Boardwalk locations are open seasonally.

KOHR BROS. FROZEN CUSTARD

(401 South Boardwalk & 112 South Boardwalk ☎ *410.289.1178* ✆ *kohrbros.com)* This frozen treat has less sugar and fat than regular ice cream, and has eggs in it. This creates a rich, custardy flavor and helps it stand up to the summer's heat a little better than ice cream. Plus, doesn't it sound healthier? Founded in 1919 on Coney Island, this family-owned business now has locations up and down the eastern seaboard, and as far afield as Arizona. The two Boardwalk locations are perfectly spaced so that frozen custard fiends can order a cone at one location and finish it in about the time it takes to stroll to the next Kohr Bros. stand.

PIEZANO'S PIZZA

(300 South Boardwalk ☎ *410.289.7433)* Piezano's thin-crust New York-style pizza really hits the spot at lunchtime on the Boardwalk. There are other places to get pizza on the Boardwalk, but Piezano's is consistently the freshest. The slices are loaded with cheese, and

the crust is light and crunchy. Their menu also includes sandwiches and subs, including a cheesesteak sub that some people swear by. Also, the service is attentive and friendly, which is a big plus on the Boardwalk where careful service is not always the case.

DOLLE'S CANDYLAND

(500 S Boardwalk at Wicomico St. & 103 120th St. ☎ *800.337.6001)* The fifth generation of the Dolle family is growing up now, while a third generation Dolle still makes nearly all the chocolates sold in the two Ocean City stores. Be sure to choose some of Mr. Dolle's truffles. You can see the difference between his homemade pieces and the factory-stamped imported truffles that are also for sale. The saltwater taffy is also the freshest and most flavorful; don't bother with any other saltwater taffy in Ocean City. All of Dolle's candies are made at their Wicomico Street location; it's fun to look in the glass door on Wicomico Street and see the small chocolate factory in action. There are other candy shops in Ocean City, but with the exception of Jessica's Fudge, also on the Boardwalk, stick to Dolle's.

JESSICA'S FUDGE HOUSE

(720 S Boardwalk ☎ *410.289.4100)* This little Boardwalk shop makes all its treats on the premises, including a huge assortment of fudge, plus chocolate-covered graham crackers, chocolate peanut butter shells, penuche, dulce de leche, and other treats that would be hugely fattening – except that you're on vacation.

BIKE RENTALS

Biking is a great way to see more of the Boardwalk, and to work off some of the fries, frozen custard, fudge, fried seafood, caramel corn, beer – well, you get the idea – that are such an integral part of an Ocean City vacation. There are plenty of bike rental shops in

Ocean City, so there will probably be one close to wherever you're staying. You can choose a sturdy beach cruiser, a recumbent bike, a tandem bike, a surrey for two or four, or even a bike with a toddler trailer. If you venture off the Boardwalk, be sure to stay in the bus lane on Coastal Highway and watch out for the big storm drains. During the high season, there are restricted hours for biking on the Boardwalk. Check the following web site for biking hours: *(⌐ beach-net.com/TownrulesOC.html)*.

There are many bike rental shops around town, and they are hard to miss. Rental shops include: **14th Street Bike Rental** *(3 14th St. ☎ 410.289.3310),* **27th St Bicycle Rental** *(☎ 410.289.6022),* **Ann's Bicycle Rental**, *(900 N Baltimore Ave. ☎ 410.289.9189),* **Bike World**, *(6 Caroline St. ☎ 410.289.2587),* **Continental Cycles** *(7203 Coastal Hwy ☎ 410.524.1313 ⌐ continentalcycles.com),* **Dandy Don's Olde Towne Bike Rentals** *(408 S Baltimore Ave. ☎ 410.289.2289),* **Fenwick Islander Bicycle Shoppe** *(RR1, Ocean View, DE ☎ 302.537.2021),* **Island Cycle, Inc.** *(106 S Baltimore Ave. ☎ 410.289.4910),* **Jo's Bikes Gifts & Collectibles** *(4 1/2 N 2nd St. ☎ 410.289.5298),* **Mike's Bikes** *(10 N Division St. ☎ 410.289.5404),* where wheelchairs are available, and **Wobbly Wheel Boardwalk Bicycle Rental** *(3 N 1st St. ☎ 410.289.2453).*

The Ocean

The jewel in Ocean City's crown is the beautiful beach. Of course, this whole book is about the many, many things to do and see in and around Ocean City – but really, the thing that brings eight million visitors here each year is the beach.

Unlike some other beach resorts, all of Ocean City's beaches are free and open to the public. They are cleaned and groomed every night, and guarded from 10:00 a.m. to 5:30 p.m. every summer day. No dogs, Frisbees, or ball playing are allowed on summer days (the beach is too crowded for that), and no private vehicles are allowed on the beach at all – except during a few off-season fishing tournaments.

Beachgoers can enjoy ten miles of wide, golden sand, and water that is bracing in June, but just barely cool in August and September. The view up and down the beach, as far as the eye can see, is of beach umbrellas, blankets, sandcastles, swimmers darting in and out of the surf, dads getting buried in the sand by their children, teenagers working on their tans, and little planes towing advertising banners in the blue sky overhead. All of this noise and activity is hushed by the endless, swirling surf.

This is the heart of the Ocean City vacation, and second and third generations of families have been trekking to Maryland's shore every summer for just this.

SURFING

The east coast is not the first place most people think of when it comes to surfing. However, Ocean City has a dedicated community of surfers who can be seen bobbing out in the water in the morning and late afternoon almost any month of the year. In the cooler months, surfers wearing slick black wetsuits look like some new kind of water mammal gathering in packs out where the waves break. In the summer, vehicles with surfboards strapped to the roof stream over the Chesapeake Bay Bridge, carrying weekend surfers from the city.

Every summer day, two or three Ocean City beaches are designated for surfing. One is always in the northern part of town, one in the central/southern part, and one (sometimes) is at the inlet. Check with the **Ocean City Beach Patrol** *(☍ town.ocean-city.md.us/ocbp/Surfing.htm)* for a complete list of the season's surfing beach schedule. You can also call any surf shop to find out where to go that day for surfing. Surfing beaches are designated with banners pitched in the sand.

Malibu's Surf Shop *(713 Boardwalk ☎ 410.289.3000 ☍ malibus.com)* and **Chauncey's** *(28th St. & Coastal Hwy ☎ 410.289.7405/ 54th St. & Coastal Hwy ☎ 410.524.6005 ☍ chaunceyssurfshop.com)* both post surf conditions on their web pages – Malibu's report is often chatty and opinionated. **K-Coast** *(35th St. & Coastal Hwy ☎ 410.524.8500 ☍ kcoast.com)* has the largest shop in town, and has sponsored the K-Coast Reef Surf Challenge every September for the last ten years.

Ocean City also has an active **Surfrider Foundation** chapter *(☍ surfrider.org/oceancitymd)*. The Surfrider Foundation is an environmental organization that works to preserve oceans and beaches. They frequently sponsor beach cleanups and dune plantings, which are surprisingly fun and sociable activities. One of Surfrider's most well-known initiatives is its weekly testing of beach water samples around the country in order to gauge water quality. You can see more information and check on the water quality of beaches around the country online. *(☍ oceans.nrdc.org)*

As more people are becoming interested in "eco-tourism," it's worth considering that the annual family trek to Ocean City could actually have a socially responsible component to it. Volunteering a few vacation hours to the Surfrider Foundation is an outstanding way to "give respect – get respect" (a Surfrider expression that actually refers to surfing etiquette) for the beautiful beaches of Ocean City.

FISHING

A huge storm created Ocean City's inlet – and Maryland's only ocean port – in 1933. In 1934, the first white marlin was caught off Ocean City's coast. This impressive fighting fish, which travels in the Gulf Stream, was known to be in the waters off the coast of Florida. It had not before been found this far north. With this discovery, sport fishermen quickly descended on Ocean City, and in 1939, over 1,000 marlins were caught. True sport fishermen started becoming alarmed about overfishing, but World War II put a stop to coastal fishing from 1942 to 1944.

After the war, marlin fishing was different. A group of marlin anglers established the Ocean City Light Tackle Club, and created a set of rules and gentlemen's agreements that limited the methods of fishing for white marlin. They also stated that only trophy or mutilated marlin would be kept, and everything else caught would be released. In 1988, federal regulations limited the number of marlin landed and kept to fish at least sixty-two inches long.

Today, deep-sea fishing enthusiasts can easily charter a boat from any of several area **charter services** *(ocean-city.com/fishing/marinas.shtml)*. The Gulf Stream, home to bigeye, yellow fin tuna, mako, blue marlin, and of course, white marlin, is easily reached in a one-day fishing trip from Ocean City. Many headboats (large charter fishing boats) and smaller charters leave at 5 a.m. and return in the late afternoon. Chartered boats have all the tackle and materials you'll need, and are staffed with experienced mates. Even if you are a complete beginner, a day of charter fishing can be a lot of fun. And in the rich waters around Ocean City, you're likely to come back with more than just stories about the one that got away. Some large headboats operate on a first-come, first-served basis, but do call ahead for reservations. That way, there's no chance you'll be left standing on the dock at 5:15 a.m.

Plenty of great fishing also happens on the Assawoman and Sinepuxent Bays as bluefish, kingfish, stripers and sea trout are plentiful. Many of the same charter boat companies that offer deep sea fishing also offer full and half-day bay trips. Again, you don't need to have any fishing experience to participate, and they'll have all the equipment you need.

Alternatively, if you are a licensed boater and bring your own tackle, you can rent a boat *(⌁ ocean-city.com/watersports)* and drift around the bay on your own. This is a great way to spend the day, whether you're fishing or not.

Recreational anglers do not need a license to fish in any of the waters around Ocean City.

THE WHITE MARLIN OPEN

(⌁ whitemarlinopen.com) Ocean City is the White Marlin Capital of the World, and host to the White Marlin Open, which occurs every first full week of August. This is the world's largest billfish tournament (billfish are large, predatory fish including swordfish and marlin). In 2008, 300 boats participated in the tournament, and over $2.2 million in prize payouts were awarded. Thousands of anglers and spectators show up for this five-day tournament.

Though the action takes place miles offshore, spectators can witness the tournament weigh-ins each evening at **Harbour Island Marina** *(14th St. & the Bay)*. People who enjoy being up for the sunrise can also watch the incredible parade of fishing vessels leaving the inlet and heading out to sea each morning. (Note: there is no parking at the marina.)

PIER AND SURF FISHING

There's always a line of anglers leaning over the railing of the Route 50 bridge as it crosses into Ocean City. This is just one of the many places to fish here. Sue Foster, owner of two area bait and tackle shops, maintains a weekly fishing report and web site *(oysterbay-tackle.com)* that includes a great list of fishing spots and some really specific advice about what kind of bait to use and what time of year to fish for different kinds of fish.

During the summer, surf fishing is allowed on Ocean City beaches before 10 a.m. and after 5:30 p.m. There are no restrictions in the off-season.

POWERBOATS, JET-SKI RENTALS, PARASAILING

The bay is a big playground on sunny summer days with power-boats and jet skis zipping back and forth across the water, flat-bottomed party boats drifting around, parasailers and even hang-gliders floating in the air above. Multiple **rental companies** *(ocean-city.com/watersports)* can outfit even beginners with all the nec-essary equipment to float – or zoom – across the bay waters.

PADDLING

Canoeing and kayaking is not a great idea on the bayside of Ocean City as you might get run over by a novice jet-skier! However, the paddling is spectacular on Assawoman Bay behind Assateague, and just north of Ocean City on the Sinepuxent Bay. It is here that you will find **Coastal Kayak** *(State Rte. 1 Fenwick Island ☎ 302.539.7999 c-kayak.com)* just north of Ocean City. They're all by themselves on the left, on the bay in the undeveloped section of Coastal Highway that goes through Fenwick Island State Park.

Other than the outfitter on Assateague Island, Coastal Kayak is the only paddling outfitter in the Ocean City area. They offer kayak and Hobie sailboat rentals and lessons. They also lead guided kayak eco-tours of Assateague as well as local salt marshes and a nearby Bald Cypress grove, which is the northernmost stand of these trees in the United States. For more experienced paddlers, they do ocean kayak tours in July and August. The bay behind Fenwick Island is a beautiful place to poke around with a kayak for an afternoon. It is generally too shallow for powerboat traffic, so it's quiet and peaceful for paddling and sailing.

Call Coastal Kayak rather than relying on their web site for guided tour specifics. Generally they do two tours a day. The itineraries they offer depend somewhat on the requests they get, so give them a call to reserve the tour you want to ensure that it'll happen.

CRABBING IN OCEAN CITY

You can go fishing or crabbing at several of Ocean City's parks. If you've never gone crabbing before, don't be intimidated. It's easy, cheap, and fun. Plus, it's one of those "authentic" beach experiences that can't be packaged and sold at an amusement park. This is a highly recommended activity for a summer afternoon.

Pack the car with a couple of beach chairs, sunscreen, a big bucket, a cooler with lunch and something to drink, and a paperback. Stop by **Rommel's Ace Hardware** *(6807 Coastal Hwy)* or any number of other stores in Ocean City to pick up some string and a crabbing net. This is an inexpensive net on a hoop a bit smaller than a basketball hoop, with a long handle. Purchase some chicken necks at any grocery store – they all sell packages of chicken parts and sometimes squid or fish for crab bait – and head to a fishing pier.

Tie some bait onto the end of a string, drop the bait end into the water, and hang onto the end or tie it onto something on the pier. You'll want to set up several lines at once in order to catch more crabs. Then relax and keep an eye on the lines. When you see the line pull taut, slowly pull the line in while easing the net into the water. If there's a crab on the line, when it reaches the surface of the water, just scoop it into the net and pull it out.

In Ocean City, crabs must measure at least five inches across from point to point (a crab's shell flares out to a point on each side.) Bring a ruler along, or this book, which is five and a half inches wide. If you catch a smaller crab, throw it back. Place any keepers in your bucket, which you have partially filled with bay water.

HOW TO COOK CRABS

When you have caught enough crabs, take them directly back to your kitchen to cook. Most rental kitchens come stocked with a big crab pot and long-handled tongs. Crab mallets and sturdy plastic crab knives are easy to pick up at local markets. Discard any crabs that have not survived the trip and drop the living crabs into a big pot of boiling water. If you'd like, add a can of beer to the crab water. *Do not cook crabs that are already dead!*

Boil the crabs for six minutes or so. While the crabs are boiling, spread newspaper on the dinner table. Or, if you have a picnic table outside, that's the best option. When the crabs are done, drop them in the middle of the table, generously sprinkle them with Old Bay Seasoning (available at any area grocery store), and dig in!

HOW TO EAT A CRAB

There are several ways to pick a Blue Crab, and most Marylanders insist that the way they were taught is the only "right" way to do it. So with apologies to any fellow Marylanders who use a different method, here is how our family does it. This is apparently also the method used in crabmeat packing plants, though that's just the family folklore:

Remove all the legs, along with the knuckle-like joints that attach them to the shell. A careful twisting motion is best. If the knuckle joint doesn't pull off with the leg, dig it out with your knife. Sometimes, a bit of meat will cling to the joint as you remove the legs. You can eat any meat that comes out with the joints.

For eating the claw meat, you'll need a crab knife and a mallet. Place the claw on the table, moveable portion down. Place the serrated edge of your knife across the claw as if you're going to chop off the non-moving portion of the claw, about ¼ inch back from the meeting of the joint. Tap on the back of your knife with your mallet until the knife has cut about halfway way through the claw. Then twist the knife so that the pincer end of the claw breaks away from the body of the claw. You should be able to remove both pincers, and with the pincers should come all the meat from the claw. Repeat the same process on the next joint up from the claw, making your cut slightly back from where that joint met the section with the pincers. You can also get a little bit out of the legs, by biting each leg in half and squeezing out the meat.

Remove the tab-like structure on the underbelly of the crab. Female crabs have a tab shaped like the Capitol dome; males are shaped like the Washington Monument.

Place the crab on the table, shell side down, mouth facing away from you. Put one hand flat on top of the crab shell. With the other hand, pick up your knife with the cutting edge facing away from the mouth, towards you. Position the knife at one edge of the crab's mouth in the open space where you pulled out the claws. Using a slight downward angle, as if you're hollowing out a shallow bowl, cut right in the center of the space where the knuckles were and saw away from the mouth, all the way around the body of the crab. Cut just deep enough for the tip of the knife to reach the center of the crab. Saw all the way around until the cutting edge of the knife meets the mouth on the other side.

Open the two halves of the crab using the mouth as a hinge. You will be presented with two halves of crab full of meat, and all the chambers that hold that meat should be cut open. Using the knife again, holding one of the halves of the crab, scoop out the meat using the tip of the knife. Eat this and enjoy! Do not eat the squiggly internal organs or the yellow "mustard" inside the crab's body.

Repeat this process until you are full, coated with Old Bay and crab gunk, and happy.

Amusements, Go-Karts, Mini-Golf

Many family amusement spots in Ocean City try to do everything. It's a mistake, however, to think that the place with the best water slide is also going to have the best mini-golf. Each place has its particular specialty, and should be appreciated for what it does best. The exception is Splash Mountain / Jolly Roger, which perhaps doesn't have the very best of everything, but it's big and it's all in one place. It also allows families who are big spenders at the Boardwalk Pier to buy a passport that covers both the Jolly Roger 30th Street Park and the Pier.

Those interested primarily in go-karts should head to West Ocean City, where the two good parks are right across the street from one another just beyond White Marlin Mall. For mini-golf, head to North Ocean City and the Delaware line, where there is a "circuit" of excellent, manicured courses that will actually be fun for all ages – adults included.

SPLASH MOUNTAIN / JOLLY ROGER AMUSEMENT PARK

(30th St. at Coastal Hwy & The Boardwalk Pier ☎ *410.289.3477 ✆ jollyrogerpark.com)* Families with children will be relieved that there is one source available for all your water slide, mini-golf and go-kart needs. Splash Mountain and the Jolly Roger Amusement Park at 30th Street will keep kids occupied all day – and parents might get hooked on the water slides, too. Jolly Roger also runs the rides and amusements on the **Boardwalk Pier**, so their Passport to Fun will be a money-saver for families who plan to spend time and money at both places. Their website has details about the Passport to Fun and other specials. Open Memorial Day through Labor Day.

65TH ST. SLIDE & RIDE

(☎ 410.524.5270 ⏢ slidenride.com) This park is a less expensive, less themed-up, and sometimes less crowded version of Splash Mountain / Jolly Roger Amusement Park. This is just fine for many parents, who would rather spend a few hours at the water amusement park, then wander over to the real beach for the free, all-natural amusements offered there. In addition to water slides and mini-golf, the 65th St. Slide & Ride also offers paint-less paintball, splash boats, a moon bounce, and bank shot basketball. Open May through September.

BAJA AMUSEMENTS

(Ocean Gateway next to White Marlin Mall ☎ 410.213.2252 ⏢ bajaoc.com) Baja and Ocean City Grand Prix are the places to go when racing is the primary goal. Baja has eight go-kart tracks: a rookie track for kids 4-7, two "family" tracks with hills and bridges, a slick track, a stock car track, and a "bullit" track built for speed. Baja Amusements also has a mini-golf course, a climbing wall, and bumper boats. Check their website for "Baja Bucks" coupons. Open seasonally.

OCEAN CITY GRAND PRIX

(Ocean Gateway across from White Marlin Mall ☎ 410.213.1278 ⏢ grandprixoc.com) With seven tracks, this is another great choice for go-kart racing for kids and adults. The park also has bumper boats, a kiddie "ball room," and a climbing wall. Open seasonally.

VIKING GOLF AMUSEMENTS & THUNDER LAGOON WATERPARK

(Coastal Hwy at Rt. 54 ☎ 302.539.1644 ⏢ vikinggolfamusements.com) The charming theme and the elaborate mini-golf course are the reasons to visit this golf, go-kart and waterpark complex just over the Delaware line. A series of skillfully carved wooden trolls lounge throughout the park for various purposes. One troll helpfully indi-

cates how tall you must be to ride the go-karts. One troll lounges on a bench, with a sign above his head asking patrons not to smoke, because the management is trying to get the trolls to quit. One has his arm stretched across the back of a bench, hoping for a cuddle. The mini-golf course, which features a huge, gnarled old tree, a waterfall, various Norse gods, and a dragon hatchery, is meticulously maintained. Signs throughout describe various Viking monsters and legends. (It's sort of educational!) You can purchase Hershey's ice cream, popcorn, and funnel cakes to snack as you golf.

GOLF DOWN UNDER

(Coastal Hwy at Rt. 54 ☎ *443.497.1931)* This is a manicured, attractive course, but not as thematically interesting as the others in the northern Ocean City mini-golf circuit. The traffic noise can be especially distracting, as the course doesn't have as much buffering greenery around its edges.

BUCCANEER'S BOOTY

(146th St. at Coastal Hwy ☎ *410.250.3888* ⏚ *buccaneersbootyoc.com)* A large game arcade and playground with a pirate ship in the sand accompany this course. This is a lush, beautifully maintained course with a waterfall and lots of tropical foliage.

PROFESSOR HACKER'S LOST TREASURE MUST SEE

(13903 Coastal Hwy ☎ *410.250.5678* ⏚ *losttreasuregolf.com)* The ultimate in manicured, themed mini-golf, Professor Hacker's Lost Treasure actually has two challenging courses – the gold and the diamond. A rush of water dumps periodically from a rusty coal car on an abandoned railroad track about two stories above ground while several holes wind through cool, dim caves. A skeleton's foot dangles over the side of a cliff next to a fraying rope ladder. An actual plane, painted bright yellow and crashed into a fake rock mountaintop, presides over the whole *Raiders of the Lost Ark*-like

affair. Signs posted throughout the park narrate the fictitious Professor Hacker's hair-raising adventures.

OLD PRO GOLF COURSES

(Various locations, Ocean City ☎ 410.524.2645 ⌖ oldprogolf.com) Seven courses, each individually themed, are generally less elaborate than the stand-alone courses in North Ocean City, though the gimmicks on each hole are sometimes sillier (treasure chests that open and shut, saber-toothed tigers that lunge at cage bars, etc.). The exception to this is their Temple of Dragons course at 23rd Street. This is a fun one to play at night, with the temple lit and glowing eerily in the dark. On a rainy day, their Indoor Golf course at 68th Street, with an underwater theme, is a great choice. Old Pro offers all-day passes for real mini-golf enthusiasts; check any of their locations for details. Open seasonally.

OCEAN DOWNS RACETRACK

(10218 Racetrack Rd. ☎ 410.641.0600 ⌖ oceandowns.com) The oldest harness track in Maryland, Ocean Downs (known as Delmarva Downs between 1988 and 1992) is just outside of Ocean City in Berlin. The track has live harness racing in June, July, and August, and simulcast races for watching and wagering year-round. Having celebrated its 60th year in 2008, Ocean Downs offers night racing—which makes things cooler in the stands—on Wednesday, Thursday, Saturday, and Sunday evenings. Post time is 7:35 p.m.

Pacers Restaurant at Ocean Downs serves dinner in its casual dining room on race nights only. Each table has its own television monitor, and a view of the Assawoman Bay. The track also has a more casual restaurant open daily, and a lounge with pool tables and a horseshoe-shaped bar. Concessions are also served in the stands.

Harness racing uses standardbred (rather than the longer-legged thoroughbred) horses, with "drivers" being pulled behind in a "sulky", which is a lightweight cart with wheels that are like bicycle wheels. Harness races often involve strategy more than speed, and the last half of the race is typically more exciting than the first, with judges having to consult finish line photographs in order to determine winners. It is useful to have a basic understanding of the race before going to Ocean Downs, and the **US Trotters Association** (🖰 *ustrotting.com/usta/newcomers.htm*) has a good beginner's overview.

Golf

Whether you're an experienced golfer or a new player looking for a fun and relatively low-pressure place to play golf, Ocean City definitely lives up to its slogan, "Close to Home and Close to Perfect." There are fifteen golf courses within an easy drive of Ocean City, and according to *Golf Digest*, at least four of them are worth the trip all by themselves. Rum Point, Ocean City Golf Club's Newport Bay course, and River Run Golf Club earned that magazine's 4-star rating, which is designated as "Outstanding. Plan your next vacation around it." The Links at Lighthouse Sound earned 4 ½ stars — with 5 stars indicating that a course is "golf at its absolute best. Pay any price to play at least once in your life." The Links at Lighthouse Sound was also named one of the "Top 100 You Can Play" by *Golf Magazine* in its ranking of the best public courses in America.

The fact that Ocean City is emerging as one of the east coast's major golfing destinations is no accident. A non-profit organization called **Ocean City Golf Getaway** (☎ *800.4OC.GOLF* ⏁ *oceancitygolf.com*) with board members from the Town of Ocean City and from the golf, restaurant, and hospitality industries, has made it easy for golf enthusiasts to cut through the many details involved in planning a golfing vacation. Contact Ocean City Golf Getaway to receive their Golf Package Planner if you are at all interested in golfing in Ocean City.

In 1990, Ocean City played fewer than 7,500 rounds of golf. In 2006, that number was nearly 300,000. This is due to the expanding number of courses and their improving quality. The jump is also surely due to how it easy now it is to book your hotel, your tee times, your lunch, and other perks with one of Ocean City Golf Getaway's participating golf packagers. Ocean City's golf courses cater to players from mid-Atlantic and New England vacationers who drive in for a few concentrated days of golf, and then head home again.

The hotel and restaurant industries have jumped on board to offer special rates and perks for people planning their vacation as part of a golf package. In addition, all the packagers have access to a central booking system, making it possible for them to lock in tee times for you. The prices a packager can get are lower than you could get if you called the golf courses or hotels yourself. Since most golf in Ocean City is played in the "shoulder" seasons of spring and fall, when hotels aren't otherwise very busy, package deals can be significant money-savers. In short, use a golf packager!

New golfers will be happy with most any of the courses in Ocean City due to the fact that almost all of them have four or five different sets of tees. Every course has lessons available with PGA professionals. Beach Club, Lighthouse Sound, and Glen Riddle have golf academies.

THE BAY CLUB

(9122 Libertytown Rd. ☎ *410.641.4081* ✆ *thebayclub.com)* The Bay Club is situated in the woodlands and wetlands west of Ocean City, providing thirty-six holes of golf on two courses. The east course offers the area's only Zoysia grass fairway. The club is relatively inexpensive, but doesn't have the stunning views or the signature course architects of some of the area's other courses.

BAYSIDE RESORT GOLF CLUB

(31806 Lakeview Dr. ☎ *302.436.3400* ✆ *golfbayside.com)* This is Delaware's first Jack Nicklaus Signature course, and serious golfers will want to include Bayside on their agendas. Located just outside of Fenwick Island off Route 54, the 18-hole course features views along the Assawoman Bay coastline and surrounding marshes, meadows, and woodlands—along with the new golf course community housing, of course. There are plans for a permanent club-

house, but for now a temporary building houses a small pro shop and outdoor bar and grill.

BAYWOOD GREENS 🔲

(32267 Clubhouse Way ☎ *302.947.9800* ⏁ *baywoodgreens.com)* This is a bit of a drive from Ocean City, but if you especially enjoy beautifully landscaped and manicured courses, this is worth the trip. Called the "Augusta of the North," Baywood Greens is an 18-hole course with eight timbered bridges, 27 acres of man-made ponds, and over 300,000 flowers, plants, shrubs and trees. The clubhouse is opulently comfortable with a hushed elegant dining room and a more casual club-like bar atmosphere, as well as comfortable dinner seating on a wide outdoor porch overlooking the greens. Take a walk up to the crow's nest at the top of the clubhouse building for a spectacular view of the whole course.

THE BEACH CLUB

(9715 Deer Park Dr. ☎ *800.435.9223* ⏁ *beachclubgolflinks.com)* As one of Ocean City's longest golf courses, this 27-hole course is divided into three distinct 18-hole, par 72 lay-outs. The links are designated as the Sand Links, the Surf Links, and the Sun Links. Long hitters will enjoy the Sand/Surf Links from the back tees.

BEAR TRAP DUNES

(7 Clubhouse Dr. ☎ *302.537.5600* ⏁ *beartrapdunes.com)* Rick Jacobson, an associate of Jack Nicklaus, designed Bear Trap Dunes to take advantages of the sandy dunes and wild coastal landscapes. This 27-hole course was listed in *Golf For Women* magazine's Top 100 Fairways. The clubhouse includes The Bistro, an upscale casual restaurant with a brick pizza oven.

EAGLE'S LANDING

(12367 Eagle's Nest Rd. ☎ *410.213.7277* ⏁ *eagleslandinggolf.com)* Along with Lighthouse Sound, this is the course that many avid

golfers familiar with Ocean City will name as a favorite. Eagle's Landing overlooks the Sinepuxent Bay and Assateague Island, and it's an Audubon Cooperative Sanctuary—the first one certified in Maryland. The 18-hole course beautifully incorporates the natural beauty of the salt marshes and seascapes. While it is a beautifully manicured course, Eagle's Landing has a more genuine feel than some golf links, which can seem (and in fact are) artificial landscapes plopped down in the middle of some farmland. Note the nest boxes scattered throughout the course. Bluebirds, mallards, purple martins, and sparrow hawks are some of the birds to be found at Eagle's Landing.

GLEN RIDDLE GOLF CLUB
(11501 Maid At Arms Way ☎ *866.441.4536* ⌂ *glenriddlegolf.com)* This club and the residential development around it were built on the site of the Riddle Farm, where the racehorses Man O' War, War Admiral, and Seabiscuit trained. A segment of the track and starting gate have been incorporated into the Man O' War track, and the clubhouse building was formerly the main stable building. The club has two golf courses: Man O' War (the public course), and War Admiral, which is currently open to the public, but will ultimately be converted to a private course. Glen Riddle is worth a visit for the sake of its fine course, and the clubhouse is worth a visit regardless of your affinity for golf. As much of the original structure as possible was saved including all the hardware and the stall doors, some of which were used as tabletops in the bar and grill area. The walls are given over to paintings, photographs, and old newspaper articles documenting the history of the farm and the famous horses it produced. Ruth's Chris Steakhouse makes its home in the former stable.

THE LINKS AT LIGHTHOUSE SOUND 🔲
(12723 St. Martin's Neck Rd., ☎ *888.55.HILLS* ⌂ *light-housesound.com)* One of the most challenging and most beautiful

courses in the Ocean City area, Lighthouse Sound overlooks the Assawoman Bay and the impressive North Ocean City skyline. Marsh, river, and bay are featured on 15 of its 18 holes, and America's longest cart bridge – nearly 1500 feet long – links the bayside to the marsh and riverside holes. The clubhouse restaurant, The Lighthouse, is very upscale, and is a beautiful spot for weddings and receptions. If you only have time to play at one course, this would be a fine choice.

OCEAN CITY GOLF CLUB'S NEWPORT BAY

(11401 Country Club Dr. ☎ 800.442.3570) Another outstanding *Golf Digest* 4-star course with beautiful bay views, Newport Bay has a policy of nine minutes between tee times to ensure that play keeps moving without delays and long waits between shots. One of Ocean City's municipal courses and one of the area's best, Newport Bay is located at the same club as the Seaside Course, which is Ocean City's oldest course, first opened in the 1950s. The two courses are very different from one another, so it's fun to play a round at each course (and they can be packaged together for savings at each.)

RIVER RUN GOLF CLUB

(11605 Masters Lane ☎ 800-733-RRUN ⌖ riverrungolf.com) This Gary Player Signature Course emphasizes the bump and run game, and it is designed to give the golfer multiple choices on each shot. The course hugs the St. Martin's River and is a beautiful place to spend a fine spring afternoon. Its Players Club Restaurant is an upscale dining destination in its own right as well. The River Run development is the only gated community on the Eastern Shore, and it seems silly to put a gate across the front entrance in such a rural, bucolic setting.

RUM POINTE

(7000 Rum Pointe Lane ☎ *888-809-GOLF* ⌂ *rumpointe.com)* Another
spectacular seaside course, Rum Pointe overlooks the Sinepuxent
Bay and Assateague National Seashore, as Eagle's Landing does.
Designed by the father/son team of Pete Dye and P.B. Dye, Rum
Pointe is another one to put on your short list. Seventeen of its 18
holes have bay views, and several have direct bay frontage. Golf
Week ranked Rum Pointe among the top 5 courses in the state.

Parks and Museums

While Ocean City is known for its clean, well-groomed sandy beaches, they also take the same meticulous care of their municipal parks. A list of all of Ocean City's parks, including several pocket parks and tot lots, can be found online. *(⌐ ococean.com/parks.html)* The same site also has a calendar of events that includes concerts and happenings at Ocean City's parks *(⌐ ocean-city.com/calendar).*

SUNSET PARK

(South Division St. on the bay) This is Ocean City's newest park, and it's a small gem of a spot. The bayside location is set up as a promenade, with views of the ocean, the bay, Assateague, and Ocean City's commercial harbor at West Ocean City. Native plants—mostly grasses—are used for landscaping, and most of the space is hardscaped with walkways and pavers. It feels like an urban park, more set up for crowds and entertainment than unstructured lounging, which is appropriate in this densely populated downtown location. This is a great place for concerts, and the city puts on plenty of them during the summer and early fall. You can go crabbing off the pier here as well, but Northside Park's pier is a more bucolic spot for that.

DORCHESTER BEACH VOLLEYBALL PARK

(On the beach between Dorchester & Talbot Sts.) Ten public volleyball courts are available for pick up volleyball games during summer daylight hours. These courts are often busy, and it's fun to hang out and watch the pickup volleyball games even if you don't play yourself. The entire beach is machine-cleaned every night so the volleyball courts are always in great shape, especially early in the day. Open seasonally.

DOWNTOWN RECREATION COMPLEX

(Between 3rd & 4th Sts. at the bay) This big recreation area is the downtown version of Northside Park. It's not as extensive, but is a great resource for residents and visitors staying downtown. The park has a lighted multi-purpose ball field along the bay, plus a playground and a small ball field for children. Basketball and tennis courts are available, with lights for evening play. A good spot for fishing and crabbing is also available at the Chicago Avenue Promenade, which is a small Boardwalk on the bay. The Ocean Bowl Skate Park is also a part of the Downtown Recreation Complex.

OCEAN BOWL SKATE PARK

(3rd St. & St. Louis Ave. ☎ *410.289.BOWL* ⌂ *oceanbowl.com)* The 17,000 square foot concrete-based park is the oldest operating municipal skate park in the United States. The park was built in 1976 and rebuilt twice since then because of wear and tear and also due to the structural damage caused by successive tropical storms. The current configuration takes advantage of every inch of space, with transitions allowing the flow from one end of the park to the other. The park contains a pool bowl, vert ramp, mini ramp and concrete street area. Skateboarders must wear helmets, knee pads and elbow pads, and inline skaters must also wear wrist guards. Skateboards are prohibited on any public property (except the skatepark) from April through September. So pack all your gear if you want to skate while you're on vacation. You must have a pass in order to use the park. Daily, weekly, and annual passes are available and a waiver signed by a parent or legal guardian is necessary. Be sure to check the web site before you go. The Ocean Bowl offers skate clinics and camps, lessons and competitions. The competitions are amazing to watch, and there is some observation seating.

NINTH STREET FISHING PIER

(9ᵗʰ St. at the bay) There are plenty of places to fish in and around Ocean City. But those who are looking for the clean convenience of fish-cleaning tables equipped with hoses will really enjoy fishing at this municipal fishing pier.

CONVENTION CENTER PARK

(41st St. at Bayside, behind the Convention Center) This is an Ocean City secret worth sharing. Behind the Convention Center is a Boardwalk promenade with benches and a small pier. This is a spectacular place for a picnic supper at sunset. On most evenings, crowds are packed into Fager's Island, Castaways, Fish Tales, and all the other bayside eateries to enjoy dinner with a sunset view. Meanwhile, the Boardwalk behind the Convention Center is often almost completely empty. Pack a gourmet supper or just pick up some carry-out, and settle in on a bench in this relaxing spot for visiting and beholding a truly spectacular sunset. You can also fish or crab off the pier, but Northside Park or the Ninth Street Fishing Pier are better bets for this.

OCEAN CITY TENNIS CENTER

(61st St. on the bay ☝ tennis.ococean.com) This USTA Tennis Welcome Center is open and professionally staffed from mid-May through mid-September. The center has a full schedule of activities on their six Premier and three Lee Fast Dry Clay courts, including leagues, tournaments, instruction, holiday mixers, clinics, and open play. Check their web site for fees; seasonal and weekly passes are available, and hourly court rental is offered. The center also offers racket rental, and racket stringing. Open seasonally.

LITTLE SALISBURY PARK / ART LEAGUE OF OCEAN CITY

(94th St. at Bayside ☝ artleagueofoceancity.org) Look for the water tower at 94th street, and tucked in next to it you will find the Art League

of Ocean City's bright turquoise and magenta building. The Art League has been active in Ocean City since the 1960s, and they offer workshops, gallery shows, and children's activities at their building and in the community. Check their web site to see what they have scheduled, and you may be able to take a nature photography workshop or a beginners' watercolor class while you're on vacation. Little Salisbury Park also has a couple of tennis courts and some basketball courts.

NORTHSIDE PARK 🟨

(125th St. on the bay) This 58-acre park has three lighted softball/baseball fields, a lighted soccer field, multipurpose field, a fishing lagoon, two playgrounds, a picnic area, two piers, a gazebo, walking/jogging paths, a large building with a gymnasium, kitchen and community room, and a sports center annex with a 21,000 square foot multi-sport sports arena. Much of this caters to Ocean City residents, who can take advantage of Ocean City's extensive recreation program schedule. However, the park is also perfect for anyone who wants to get out and toss a baseball around, or shoot some hoops, or take the kids to a couple of big playgrounds with great bay views. The fishing pier is definitely the place to go for an afternoon of crabbing in a rural, family-friendly setting. There's a gazebo at about mid-point on the pier that provides welcome shade on sunny days.

Shopping and Day Spas

Ocean City is not known as a shopping destination, though the gigantic outlet shopping malls in Rehoboth are not far away. The stores that are in Ocean City are generally small, locally owned shops. So if you're looking for a shopping experience that's actually quite different from what's available at home, you'll be interested in several shops, listed here.

Some stores close during the winter, but the "closed" season seems to be getting shorter and shorter in Ocean City. Still, the selections are mostly limited in January and February.

CLOTHING

In addition to the stores listed below, cute beach clothing can be found in the surf shops, described in this book's surfing section.

QUIET STORM

(7409 Coastal Hwy ☎ *410.723.1313* ✆ *quietstormshop.com)* This two-level shop has young, surf-inspired clothes and shoes for men and women. Part of a small chain with stores in Maryland, South Carolina, Florida, Hawaii, and the U.S. Virgin Islands, the shop sells such brands as Quicksilver, Billabong, O'Neil, and Tommy Bahama. Open year round.

SEA QUEST

(7503 Coastal Hwy ☎ *410.524.0076)* Sea Quest is known for its large selection of swimwear. They claim they can fit anybody! They also carry a large selection of resort clothing, and if it weren't for South Moon Under, Sea Quest would be the most unique clothing store at the beach. As it is, it suffers by comparison because it is just as pricy, but doesn't do as fine a job with its displays or its variety. Also, Sea Quest does not carry men's clothing. Still, for the

shopper who is looking for resort clothing that's refreshingly different from the usual department store choices, Sea Quest is definitely worth a visit. Open year round.

SOUTH MOON UNDER

(8019 Coastal Hwy ☎ *410.524.4567* ⌁ *southmoonunder.com)* The owner of this unusual, high-end clothing store for men and women opened an Ocean City surfboard shop in a shack in 1968, with some beach clothing strung up as an afterthought. Now, South Moon Under is an upscale clothing retailer with about a dozen stores selling really fresh, unusual fashions in Maryland, Pennsylvania, and Virginia. While the men's section is smaller, the store features dozens of names in designer clothing, swimwear, and an irresistible selection of shoes. The shop also includes an assortment of beach-themed picture frames and candles, soaps and bar accessories. Open year round.

BOOKSTORES

Lounging under a beach umbrella and reading paperbacks is a time-honored vacation tradition. Fortunately, several good local book shops will keep you stocked—new, used, and bargain stores are all to be found right in Ocean City.

ATLANTIC BOOKS

(101 Coastal Hwy ☎ *302.537.1911* ⌁ *atlanticbooks.us)* The largest and best bookshop serving Ocean City, Atlantic Books – just over the Delaware line on the ocean side in Fenwick – stocks plenty of remaindered and bargain-priced books, as well as a big selection of regular-priced books in all subject areas. They always have a display of books about the mid-Atlantic beach resorts, and an irresistible assortment of mysteries and great beach reads. Open year round.

THE BOOKSHELF, ETC.

(8006 Coastal Hwy ☎ 410.524.2949) This place features a jumble of used books, including lots of romances and mysteries perfect for beach reading. Many are sold at half of their cover price, making The Bookshelf expensive as used bookstores go. Its ocean side, upper midtown location is convenient, but its selection and pricing are not as good as the other used bookstore further uptown. Hours vary seasonally.

THE BOOK STORE AT BAYSIDE PLAZA

(13719 Coastal Hwy ☎ 410.250.1385) This is a well-stocked and well-organized used bookstore, with fair pricing and a wide range of subjects. It's always worth browsing their sidewalk sale display as well, especially if you're already at the Bayside Plaza to visit Cefaloni's Italian Deli.

HALLMARK NEWS CENTER

(118th St. & Coastal Hwy ☎ 410.524.0547 / White Marlin Mall, West Ocean City ☎ 410.213.1440) Bookshelves cover about half of the floor space in these large card and gift shops. Both stores carry bestsellers and good selections of popular fiction, as well as regional interest titles, cookbooks, self-help, religious, and children's books. They also have the widest assortment of magazines available in Ocean City. Open year round.

BEACH SUPPLIES/GIFTS/SOUVENIRS

You're going to need sunscreen for the beach. You may also need a souvenir Christmas ornament for the grandparents, a fun new toy for the kids, or perhaps a driftwood sculpture for the living room to remind you of summer vacation on dreary winter days. In addition to the blocks and blocks of t-shirt and souvenir shops on the

Boardwalk, here are some unique spots to consider when you want to pick up beach gear or a special memento.

CHRISTMAS SPIRIT

(3400 Coastal Hwy ☎ 410.289.6101) This large Christmas store, housed in a charming two-story barn building, has an amazing variety of Christmas ornaments and decorations, along with a selection of candles and non-seasonal gifts. Mostly, though, it's all about Christmas ornaments: shell-themed ornaments; Santas in Hawaiian beach trunks; ornaments in the shapes of hot dogs, burgers, pizza, and fries; mermaid and mermen ornaments; and flamingo ornaments, plus crèches, stockings, and Advent calendars. Open year-round.

DONALD'S DUCK SHOPPE

(Gold Coast Mall on 11515 Coastal Hwy ⌁ donaldsduckshoppe.com) This shop has a large selection of high-end gifts, souvenirs, stained glass, beach-themed sculptures and décor items. Items for purchase include tide clocks, ships lanterns, and decorative ships wheels. So if you want to find a well-crafted nautical-themed collectible to take home for a Christmas gift or to decorate your own home, Donald's Duck Shoppe is the right place. The prices reflect the high quality of craftsmanship generally found in the shop. Open year round.

MADE BY HAND INTERNATIONAL COOPERATIVE

(Rt. 1, York Beach Mall ☎ 302.539.6335) This store carries a thoughtful selection of clothing, baskets, pottery, jewelry, children's toys and gifts, and small musical instruments like rattles and djembe drums. All items are fair-traded from around the world, and the shop includes extensive information about the provenance of all of its goods. Open year round.

POTTERY PLACE/PERKS CAFÉ

(Sunshine Plaza, Rt. 1 ☎ 302.539.3603 ⌂ potteryplaceperks.com) This sprawling pottery and gift shop just north of the Delaware line on the bayside has a funky mixture of upscale, beachy home accessories and gifts. It also has an espresso bar tucked in the back where one should just skip the packaged baked goods, and enjoy a coffee or espresso drink instead. These are the real deal. Open year round.

ROSE'S

(200 94th St.) This discount department store has clothing and shoes, beach chairs and towels, furniture and cleaning supplies and patio furniture and toys. The quality of their merchandise is all over the map, and you never know what might be in stock – but that's what makes a trip to Rose's something like a treasure hunt. The supply of wind chimes made out of shells and Ocean City sweatshirts is pretty much guaranteed, and anything else you find that works for you is a nice bonus. Plus, everything is so inexpensive that if you make a mistake (that sundress with the fringy appliqués isn't going to work for you after all?), then it's no big deal.

SUNSATIONS

(13 Ocean City locations ☎ 800.786.9044) Sunsations sells fun, inexpensive beach gear such as beach chairs, umbrellas, boogie boards, and beach towels for your stay. They also have bathing suits, tons of beach-themed t-shirts and sweatshirts, flip-flops, shell bracelets, sunscreen, and the like. Don't expect high quality, durable merchandise here – at these prices, consider Sunsations stuff to be practically disposable.

GROCERS

If you're staying in Ocean City for more than a day or two, eventually you'll need to buy some food at someplace other than a restaurant.

FOOD LION

(11801 Coastal Hwy ☎ *410.524.9039)* If you need a big, fully stocked supermarket, this is your best bet. The store is large and clean, and the produce is fresher than the other grocery stores in town. They also have a good selection of organic and ethnic items.

CEFALONI'S ITALIAN DELI

(Bayside Plaza, 138th St. & Coastal Hwy ☎ *410.250.5696)* If you have rented a condo, or a hotel room with a kitchen, this is the place to go to stock it with some genuine Italian deli cold cuts, pasta and sauce, and other traditional Italian fare. You can also get whole trays of lasagna and homemade meatballs to serve from your own kitchen. Or, order sub sandwiches on sub rolls that are round rather than oblong: one sub easily feeds two people. This is a real find in a city with plenty of great Italian restaurants, but few options for stocking your kitchen for meals at "home." Open seasonally.

MCCABE'S GOURMET MARKET

(York Beach Mall ☎ *302.539.8550* ⌂ *mccabesgourmet.com)* This upscale deli is worth the drive from anywhere in the Ocean City area. They have an extensive selection of gourmet cheese, as well as fresh baguettes, bagels, and other baked goods, deli meats and several delicious pasta salads every day. They have a small, but excellent selection of groceries, including pastas and pasta sauces, dairy products, high-quality fruit juices, and other healthy things for your beach kitchen. The espresso and coffee drinks are also excellent.

McCabe's is also the best place to go for really fine picnic fare. Open year round.

OCEAN CITY FARMERS MARKET

(142nd St. & Coastal Hwy ⌕ atbeach.com/farmersmarket) Ocean City isn't the first place one thinks of for healthy, fresh foods. So it may come as a surprise, then, that it boasts a 4-day-per-week farmers market all the way through the summer season. The market is full of fresh, local produce from Eastern Shore farmers, and even some organic fruits and veggies. This is a much better option for stocking the beach rental fridge than most of the grocery stores in the Ocean City proper, which are marginal at best when it comes to produce. May-October: Sundays, Tuesdays, Thursdays, and Saturdays 8 a.m. to 1 p.m.

OCEAN CITY ORGANICS

(11944 Ocean Gateway ⌕ oceancityorganics.com) This the only organic grocery store in town. The selection of produce is small but fresh, and they have an assortment of their own brand of rice, muesli, and other delicious, grainy things in small packages that are just right for a few days or a week. In another room, the store also carries health-related books, gifts, and sundries, vitamins, candles, toiletries, and a small selection of organic wines. Open year round.

SEASIDE DELI MARKET

(73rd St. & Coastal Hwy ☎ 410.524.7207) If you are fortunate enough to be renting a condo within walking distance of the Seaside Deli Market, then you're all set. This little market has a little bit of everything: homemade soups, salads, sandwiches, and coffee, plus a big deli case where you can buy cold cuts, pasta salads, even devilled eggs with Old Bay sprinkled on top. They also have beer, wine, and ice, and a small, but useful selection of grocery and dairy items. Open seasonally.

DAY SPAS

Relaxing is easy in Ocean City, on the warm sand with the sound of the ocean a soothing constant. However, the beach can wreak havoc on hair, skin, and nails. There are some good spa choices in Ocean City, listed here, for those of you who want to look and feel fabulous from head to toe while you enjoy your time at the beach.

CREATIVE HAIR, SKIN, AND NAILS

(13717 Coastal Hwy ☎ 410.250.8664 ⌁ creativedayspa.com) This small day spa has been in business in Ocean City for twenty years. Though it is located in a nondescript bayside strip mall location in North Ocean City, its pretty moss and plum décor and friendly staff make this a comfortable place to go for everything from a haircut to a massage, or a manicure, or a facial. They carry Institut Esthedern, OPI, and Paul Mitchell products, among others. Recent seasonal specials included pumpkin spice facials and pumpkin body wraps. Open year round.

A PERFECT FACE DAY SPA

(12638 Ocean Gateway Village ☎ 410.213.9883 ⌁ aperfectface.com) This is the largest most comprehensive, upscale day spa in the Ocean City area. With its opulent and warm décor, this is a "destination spa" rather than a place to stop in for a quick manicure. Services include skincare, massage, hair, nails, makeup, threading, reflexology, and even a menu of children's services. Check their web site for seasonal specials. Open year round.

VISIONS DAY SPA

(12207 Coastal Hwy ☎ 410.250.5188 ⌁ visionsdayspa.com) Visions shares a parking lot with Hooters Restaurant, but don't let that scare you off. Visions is an upscale, professional spa with a surprising variety of services. In addition to the usual menu of massage, manicures, and haircuts, Visions offers reflexology, ear candling,

acupuncture, and couples massage. Ear candling is especially sooth-ing after a few days of ocean swimming. Open year round.

Restaurants

Eating out is a big vacation pastime. So it's no surprise that Ocean City is packed full of restaurants. The town can't seem to get enough of Italian food, breakfast places, and steak and seafood restaurants. You won't find better crabcakes, sub sandwiches, or creamed chip beef on toast anywhere. (Creamed chip beef on toast has been raised to an art form in Ocean City.)

If you're looking for healthy fare, vegetarian food, or ethnic cuisine, you'll have to dig a little deeper. If eating healthy is a particular passion, it would be wise to rent a condo with a full kitchen and plan to do some cooking.

The other thing Ocean City has in spades is places to drink. Most of the nicer restaurants – and many of the dives – have bars in them. Then there are the actual bars just for drinking. In all, there are over 120 places to go and be served a drink within Ocean City's limits. And that doesn't count the liquor stores.

The dress code in Ocean City is, in a word, casual. Even at the finest restaurants, men can wear their nicest Hawaiian shirt and khakis. Women in summery sundresses are welcome anywhere. However, women who enjoy getting all dressed up for a night on the town should go for it. It's not uncommon to see a couple out for a night on the town with him sporting a funky Hawaiian shirt and slouchy pants, and her wearing a cocktail dress and strappy sandals. There's really no right or wrong, especially considering that in the summertime, everyone is a tourist and there's no reason to try and look like a blasé local.

Price ranges are approximate, and are noted as follows: *"$" = inexpensive (less than $10 per entrée), "$$" = moderate ($10 to $20 per entrée), "$$$" = expensive (more than $20 per entrée).* Contact the restaurant for their seasonal schedule.

BREAKFAST

Many restaurants have breakfast on their menu. The restaurants listed here are the places that specialize in the care and feeding of hungry and possibly hung over people in the morning. There are a couple of restaurants that really cross the line from lunch place to notable breakfast spot. Their reviews are with the other lunch/dinner establishments, but they deserve a nod here, too. First, The Crabcake Factory, USA has a great breakfast menu that includes lump crab Benedict, a light, fresh, grilled veggie pita, and assorted omelettes. Also, Anthony's Carryout, known mainly for their roast beef sandwiches, also makes excellent – and large – breakfast sandwiches with egg, cheese, bacon, or sausage.

BAYSIDE SKILLET

(7701 Coastal Hwy ☎ *410.524.7950* ✆ *baysideskillet.com)* Strawberry Shortcake must have been the interior decorator for this popular breakfast place. Painted pink on the outside, this establishment is liberally decorated with strawberry motifs and cheery shades of red and pink on the inside. But don't worry if the décor isn't working for you. The crepes and omelets are light and delicious, the fresh-squeezed orange juice is terrific, and the service is fast and friendly. Sit under a shaggy pink umbrella on the bayside deck if the weather is nice. ($)

THE BREAKFAST CAFÉ   ⋂0

(42736 Ocean Gateway ☎ *410.213.1804)* This little breakfast place on Route 50 in West Ocean City looks really cute from the outside, with its tiny wooden deck and cheerfully painted "omelettes" sign. Inside, though, the floor is sticky, the coffee is weak, and the breakfast is nothing memorable. ($)

CAFFE CAFÉ

(Gold Coast Mall ☎ *410.524.2233* ✆ *caffecafe.net)* A nice spot to sit outside with a cup of coffee or espresso and a pastry, this little shop also serves smoothies, a few breakfast sandwiches, and desserts that are perfect for an afternoon snack. ($)

FRACTURED PRUNE   *donuts oily, small grease balls.*

(2908 Philadelphia Ave. / North Bay Shopping Ctr. at 127th St. ✆ *Fracturedprune.com)* In 1976, the owner of this unique donut shop purchased a mini-market on 46th Street. In the abstract of the land he had just bought, the name Prunella Shriek appeared as a landowner in the late 1800s. In researching Ocean City history, he learned that Prunella Shriek, though in her seventies, competed with men in traditionally men's sports like ice skating races and skiing competitions. Often she would return from these competitions in a wheelchair or on crutches, and townspeople affectionately referred to her as "Fractured Prunella." The owner was inspired to name his business after her, and the two Ocean City Fractured Prune donut shops that now exist were born out of this original 46th Street location (which no longer exists).

Let's get to the important part, though: these are the freshest, tastiest donuts in Ocean City by a mile. Customers can watch the donuts rolling off the simple donut-making machine, and see them get hand-dipped to order. At the peak of the summer season, a Fractured Prune shop cranks out as many as 46 dozen donuts an hour. They're only open from 8 a.m. until 11 a.m., and sometimes there's a line clear out the door. Don't worry about that: the line moves quickly and these hot, delicious donuts are well worth the wait. They are smallish, light and tender, not dense and cakey like most donuts. The shops also have fun specialty dips and glazes, like the O.C. Sand donut, which is honey glazed with cinnamon and sugar. Others include the Ms. Prunella, with a mixed berry glaze and cinnamon sugar, and the Banana Nut Bread, with banana glaze, cinnamon sugar, and peanuts. ($)

THE GENERAL'S KITCHEN

(7400 Coastal Hwy ☎ *410.723.0477)* This breakfast spot at the Beachmark Motel is a favorite of locals and many tourists who have been returning here every year for decades. The signature decorating item in this cozy, faded dining room is the series of slightly dusty baseball caps that line the walls. Their signature special is Creamed Chipped Beef, though, frankly, they taste a bit floury. However, their typical breakfast plates are well-executed, classic diner favorites, such as eggs, toast, hash browns, grits, and all the coffee you can drink. There is usually a line during the summer season, but it moves quickly. ($)

HAPPY JACKS PANCAKE HOUSE

(504 Philadelphia Ave. ☎ *410.289.7377)* This large, popular pancake place deserves the big crowds it draws. The service is friendly and attentive, and the food is simple, fresh, and tasty with no unpleasant surprises (so distressing at breakfast.) They know how to cook eggs correctly to order, which is rare. Over easy and over medium are two different things and Happy Jacks understands the distinction. Two unusual menu items are buckwheat pancakes and sweet potato pancakes. Both are delicious, and the sweet potato pancakes have a hint of cinnamon and nutmeg. They're tasty together, and you pair them up by ordering a side of each. Happy Jack also makes great creamed chipped beef, with large pieces of the thin beef with a rich, flavorful white gravy. The coffee is fresh and strong, too. ($)

JAVA BEACH CAFÉ

(210 Talbot St.) In the oldest part of Ocean City, little clapboard bungalows still line some blocks. One has been turned into a charming, tiny ice cream shop and coffee spot, with a few tables and chairs inside and a homey, but not too cutesy, old-town feel.

The shop also has packaged chips and snacks to carry out. Open seasonally. ($)

LAYTON'S

(1601 Philadelphia Ave. ☎ *410.289.6635/9204 Coastal Hwy* ☎ *410.524.4200)* Skip this local breakfast place. While some are loyal to it because it's an Ocean City tradition, visits to both locations have yielded weak coffee, overcooked eggs, watery grits, and indifferent service. The downtown location makes their own donuts, but if it's fresh donuts you're after you'll find better at The Fractured Prune. ($)

THE LITTLE HOUSE OF PANCAKES, RIBS & PIZZA

(73rd St. & Coastal Hwy ☎ *410.520.0407)* Visit this little restaurant, for its niche is pancakes: chocolate chip pancakes, banana walnut pancakes, and even bacon pancakes (with little pieces of bacon mixed into the batter). The dining room is small and bustling, but it's smoothly run and comfortable, like a local version of a Denny's. They have patio seating in warm weather. Come here for breakfast as better pizza and ribs can be had elsewhere in town. ($)

LUNCH AND FAST, CASUAL FARE

Subs shops are a dime a dozen in Ocean City, and most will satisfy your hunger and get you back out on the beach or mini-golf course without much fuss. Then there's the Philly Cheesesteak phenomenon. Philadelphia vacationers won't need to worry about cheesesteak withdrawal in Ocean City. Multiple pizza and sub shops sell them, and cheesesteak aficionados debate about which is best. True, it's not as weighty a question as who makes the best crabcake—but it's certainly an issue in town. Depending on who you ask, **Tommy's** *(2900 Philadelphia Ave.* ☎ *410.289.6650)* or **Pizza Tugo's** *(two Ocean City locations* ☎ *410.524.2922* ⌂ *ocean-*

[handwritten note] — exceptionally long wait, food avg @ best, staff clueless and inefficient.

city.com/pizzatugos), or **Caruso** *(Boardwalk at Wicomico* ☎
410.289.1990 ✆ *ocean-city.com/caruso.htm)*, or **Biggie's** *(1804 Philadelphia Ave.* ☎ *410.289.3222)* do Philly cheesesteaks right. For sci-
entific purposes, you might have to sample each of them to find
your own favorite. There are other tasty choices for lunch and fast
fare as well.

ANTHONY'S CARRYOUT

(1608 N Philadelphia Ave. ☎   *410.289.9193)* Expect to wait in line
and pay a premium for a roast beef or other deli sandwich at Anthony's. And you will not regret either the wait or the money. The
roast beef sandwich, especially, is legendary. Portions are large, and
the meat is fresh, tender, and delicious. ($)

BELLY BUSTERS

(45th St. & Coastal Hwy ☎ *410.524.7116)* This locals' favorite lives
up to its name, with big, meaty crabcakes, generously sized subs,
and specials on clams, shrimp, or wings and pitchers of beer. The
tap at the little tiki-style bar recently included Blue Moon, Fosters,
and Yuengling. Belly Buster's patio is nothing fancy, and it sits right
out on the busy Coastal Highway, but in season it fills up each evening with friendly, hungry folks who often stick around to social-
ize. The restaurant also sells cases of beer to take home. ($)

DUMSER'S DAIRYLAND

(601 S Atlantic Ave. ☎ *410.289.0934 / 4901 Coastal Hwy* ☎
410.524.1588 / 12305 Coastal Hwy ☎ *410.250.5543* ✆ *beach-
net.com/dumsers)* This fun, 1950s-style local chain is famous for its
soft-serve ice cream cones on the Boardwalk. Their restaurants,
though, are full-service ice cream parlors. You can also grab a traditional American-style dinner of fried chicken or an open-faced
roast turkey sandwich. Make sure, though, to leave room for a ba-

nana split, a rich, generous milkshake, or in the summertime, strawberry shortcake with fresh berries. ($)

FAT DADDY'S

(82nd St. & Coastal Hwy ☎ *410.524.8228 / 216 S Baltimore Ave.* ☎ *410.289.4040* ☐ *Fatdaddysocmd.com)* Designated the best pizza on the Eastern Shore in 2008 by *Baltimore Magazine*, Fat Daddy's knows how to make a good pizza. And furthermore, they're not afraid to put absolutely anything on it. One house specialty is the Italian Pesto pizza: a crispy crust topped with tomato pesto, mozzarella, pit ham, Genoa salami, cappicola, onions, and basil pesto with essentially a salad thrown on top of it, dressing and all. This is delicious for about five minutes, and then the dressing soaks in and makes a mess of the whole thing. But this problem is easily solved by asking for the dressing on the side. Another equally improbable specialty is the Fad Daddy: a pizza topped with marina sauce, roast beef, onions, peppers, hot relish, cheddar, mozzarella, barbeque sauce, and – french fries. Bottled beers include Magic Hat, Acme, Arrogant Bastard Ale, Brooklyn Pennant Ale, Stella Artois, and others. Every surface in Fat Daddy's downtown location is completely covered with graffiti. The 82nd Street location is clean and new, and has signs prominently posted that prohibit graffiti anywhere on the premises. ($)

LOMBARDI'S

(94th St. Shopping Center, Coastal Hwy ☎ *410.524.1961* ☐ *lombardis-restaurant.com)* Most locals prefer Lombardi's pizza, because it is a traditional, crisp, simple pizza with no gimmicks. Lombardi's also has a full menu of old-fashioned Italian favorites, including spaghetti and meatballs, lasagna, and eggplant parmesan. For those who must eat crab at every meal while on vacation in Ocean City, Lombardi's serves linguini with crab meat during the summer season. ($)

OC KABOB & GRILL

(Gold Coast Mall ☎ 410-524-5524 ⌂ ockabobgrill.com) A small, pretty café in the Gold Coast Mall with Mediterranean fare that includes grape leaves, hummus, baba ghanouj, and other light snacks. ($)

CASUAL LUNCH AND DINNER

Casual restaurants in Ocean City are heavy on the seafood—crabcakes, in particular—but there are also many other options: Mexican fare, Irish pub food, Italian pizza and spaghetti, ribs, traditional American fare, and even a few Middle Eastern and Asian choices. This is just a small sampling of the hundreds of casual dining choices in Ocean City.

ANGLER RESTAURANT

(312 Talbot St. ☎ 410.289.7424) The free coastline cruise at 7 or 9 p.m. that comes with dinner may be reason enough to visit this Ocean City landmark, which dates back to 1939. The menu focuses on fresh fish specials and diners can order any number of daily catches in one of seven different ways. The restaurant is large, a bit threadbare, and impersonal in the way that big tourist places can be. But the dockside setting is authentic, and the boat ride is a nice bonus. ($$$)

BJ'S ON THE WATER

(75th St. on the Bay ☎ 410.524.7575 ⌂ bjsonthewater.com) This bar and restaurant has the friendliness and the attic-chic décor that places like Ruby Tuesday's aim for, but miss. Steaks and seafood specials dominate the menu, and sports events are always on the multiple bar TVs. BJ's has live entertainment with no cover each Wednesday, Friday, and Saturday night. Staff feed the ducks on the bay each day at 1 p.m. from the back deck. BJ's sponsors an annual canoe race on the bay each July, which is more about laughing and

cheering for the paddlers than it is about actually racing canoes. ($$)

THE BLUE BOX/BABE'S BLUE OX STEAKHOUSE & RAW BAR

(127th St. & Coastal Hwy ☎ *410.250.6440* ♙ *babesoc.com)* Happy hour brings out the local crowd at this bar that looks like a very upscale rumpus room. With its mismatched coffeehouse-like seating and its big steel-topped bar, the décor has a fun, urban eclectic feel to it. Some of the appetizers on the menu try too hard to be chic. Such as the sesame seed-encrusted tuna nachos with wonton chips, seaweed salad, and red chili and wasabi mayo which was just silly. The kitchen knows how to turn out a great steak, though, and the after-work crowd is always loud and friendly. ($$)

BULL ON THE BEACH-94TH ST.

(94th St. & Coastal Hwy ☎ *410.524.2455 / 211 Atlantic Ave.* ☎ *410.289.2855* ♙ *bullonthebeachoc.com)* These casual sports-bar restaurants specialize in pit beef sandwiches, open pit-grilled steaks, and seafood. They offer fish seared over an open flame as a nod to their signature open pit style, as well as a raw bar and a large beer selection. ($$)

CAFÉ MIRAGE

(12827 Coastal Hwy ☎ *410.250.6472)* A Mediterranean bistro specializing in North African and middle-eastern cuisine, Café Mirage is a nice break from heavy, fried beach food. Its specialty is grilled kebabs, stuffed grape leaves, hummus, and flat breads baked daily in the restaurant's clay oven. The homemade saffron rosemary ice cream is an unusual treat. ($)

CRAB ALLEY

(9703 Golf Course Rd. ☎ *410.213.7800* ♙ *craballey.com)* A West Ocean City favorite among families and big groups out for a tradi-

tional crab feast. Crab Alley's crabs are heavy and perfectly spiced, and the service is great – which is important especially when there are a dozen or more people in your party and you're doing the all-you-can eat feast (which is recommended).

THE CRABCAKE FACTORY USA

(12000 Coastal Hwy ☎ *410.250.4900* ⏻ *crabcakefactoryusa.com)* It is dangerous business to declare that one restaurant has the best crabcake in Ocean City, because different people look for different things in this ultimate, local treat. Having said that, The Crabcake Factory makes a truly spectacular crabcake. Choose between "regular" and "all-lump," (either is excellent) and get a crabcake that is tender, cooked perfectly through, and not too salty or overwhelmed by Old Bay. The simple preparation is just right because the crabmeat used is of the very highest quality. The Crabcake Factory also makes its own tasty potato chips. ($$)

DUFFY'S TAVERN 🏛️

(12923 Coastal Hwy ☎ *410.250.1449* ⏻ *duffysoc.com)* Hearty Irish food may not be the first thing you think of when you consider beach vacations. However, Duffy's Tavern will change your mind about that, and you'll come back every time you visit Ocean City. In addition to the usual American bar fare, (chili, wings, nachos, etc.) they serve shepherd's pie, corned beef and cabbage, and genuine, delicious bangers and mashers. It goes without saying that the bar's tap includes Guinness and other Irish beers. ($)

FISH TALES

(22nd St. and the Bay ☎ *410.289.7438* ⏻ *ocfishtales.com)* Adults and kids alike will enjoy Fish Tales, with its swings and sandy outdoor seating area, its outdoor play area for kids, and its brightly colored umbrellas and Adirondack chairs. A part of the Bahia Marina, Fish Tales is a great place to while away a lazy afternoon watching the traffic on the bay, or a nice finish to a day of boating. This is truly a

family-friendly establishment, in that it is truly appealing for the adults in the family as well as the kids. ($$)

GROVE MARKET

(12402 Saint Martins Neck Rd. ☎ *410.352.5055)* This funky hole-in-the-wall in Bishopville, just west of Ocean City over the Route 90 bridge, may turn out to be the best restaurant you visit during your trip to Ocean City. It looks like a small, run-down roadhouse in the woods. Despite this (or maybe because of it), you must make reservations weeks in advance during the summer season. There are no menus and the staff will tell you what's available that day. Seafood and fresh, local ingredients make up the restaurant's offerings, which also include a very respectable wine list. Dress down, turn your cell phone off, bring cash only, and leave the kids at home. If you can abide by all these restrictions, Grove Market will knock your socks off. ($$$)

THE ISLAND CAFÉ

(13729 Coastal Hwy ☎ *410.250.2939)* Another bayside strip mall find, The Island Café has been called the home of Ocean City's best crabcakes by some. Others swear they have the best steak and cheese sub. This is definitely a neighborhood favorite, and it looks like a cross between a hotel bar and a Friendly's restaurant, with a nondescript décor that makes few "island" references. Their fried green beans is a fun happy hour snack. ($)

J/RS FOR RIBS

(6104 Coastal Hwy ☎ *410.524.7427 / 131st St. & Coastal Hwy* ☎ *410.250.3100)* One local called J/Rs the "Dough Roller for ribs." Interpret this in two ways: it's not the best place, but it is fast, family-friendly, and not too pricy. The ribs are fattier than those at J/Rs, and some say they make an excellent crabcake, though it's not their specialty. ($$)

LA HACIENDA

(8003 Coastal Hwy ☎ *410.524.8080* ✆ *lahaciendaoc.com)* There's an oil painting of a naked lady matador hanging over the bar at La Hacienda. It is perhaps the only reason to visit this overpriced, overhyped Mexican cantina. The chips are cold, and the salsa tastes like it came from a jar. In a "La Ha" hard taco, the beans are flavorless, the tomatoes are mealy, and the iceberg lettuce is limp. Strawberry margaritas are an alarming shade of neon red and seem to be devoid of alcohol. If you're itching for some tasty Mexican food, Tequila Mockingbird is a much better bet. ($$)

MARINA DECK RESTAURANT

(306 Dorchester St. ☎ *410.641.5590* ✆ *Marinadeckrestaurant.com)* Known for their cream of crab soup (you can practically stand a spoon up in it), their coconut muffins (sweet and rich), and their friendly service, the Marina Deck is a comfortable, old Ocean City standard. In addition to local seafood specials, ask about the lobster they import from Canada. The staff says Canadian lobsters are bigger than anything you can get from Maine waters. The large, weathered wooden bar overlooks the docks at the inlet, and there is nothing more relaxing than having a drink and watching the sun set over the working bayside docks of Ocean City. ($$)

NICK'S HOUSE OF RIBS

(14410 Coastal Hwy ☎ *410.250.1984* ✆ *nickshouseofribs.com)* If you're looking for ribs, there are several choices in Ocean City. Nick's is the best for ribs that are flavorful and not overly sloppy with sauce (though extra sauce is yours for the asking here.) The décor is sports-themed, and the wait can be extensive – 60 to 90 minutes in season. Arrive early to minimize waiting times, and enjoy a drink at the large and friendly bar to help pass the time until your table is ready. ($$)

OC FROGS

(806 S Atlantic Ave. in the Inlet Village ☎ *410.289.2850)* This little bar and grill, tucked at the back of the shops at the inlet end of the Boardwalk, has great burgers and flounder sandwiches, and it is surprisingly not so crowded. A house specialty is the seafood club sandwich, with crabcake, shrimp salad, bacon, and provolone. The view of the inlet is spectacular, and if you drive, you can park for free in OC Frog's private parking lot directly beneath the restaurant (don't enter the inlet parking lot. Parking is validated by OC Frog's, so it's not free for others.) ($)

ON THE BAY SEAFOOD 🔲

(4204 Coastal Hwy ☎ *410.524.7070* 🖱 *onthebayseafood.net)* This is the quintessential shack at the beach where you can take your family for a crab feast on brown paper at a picnic table with sand underfoot. The husband-and-wife owners pour their energy into this tiny, freshly clean place, and it's obvious. Large parties can reserve the long VIP picnic table, designated in hand-painted red lettering on the end of the table. Everything is shipshape and coated in fresh, jaunty red and white paint. There is a tank in the waiting area where we watched a crab as it shed its shell; then we ordered that crab as a soft-shell crab sandwich. One the Bay's crabs are trucked up daily from the owners' crabbing operation in North Carolina. Open seasonally. ($$)

PLAZA TAPATIO

(12534 Ocean Gateway ☎ *410.213.7324* 🖱 *plazatapatia.com)* One of a successful local chain of Mexican restaurants, Plaza Tapatia serves traditional—if somewhat bland—Mexican fare. Their chips and salsa are fresh and tasty, but avoid the white dipping sauce they also put on the table, which is reminiscent of Miracle Whip. They also have locations in Easton and Cambridge, on the way to and from the beach. ($)

SEACRETS 🆒

(49ᵗʰ St. & the Bay ☎ *410.524.4900* ✎ *seacrets.com)* This is the biggest, most popular club for twenty-somethings in Ocean City (more about this in the Nightlife section.) Seacrets has a Jamaican theme, and the lunch and dinner fare is surprisingly good. The jerk chicken is spicy and flavorful, though that is their only nod to authentic Caribbean cuisine. Green salads are always fresh, and the seafood dishes are prepared with a light hand, allowing the clean, fresh tastes to shine through. Wooden booth seating is arrayed under palm trees in the sand, overlooking the bay. ($$)

SUNSET GRILLE

(12933 Sunset Ave. ☎ *410.213.8110* ✎ *ocsunsetgrille.com)* One evening of any Ocean City vacation should be spent in West Ocean City, as this is where much of the newest and most upscale development is happening, and it's focused on the commercial docks. The views from Sunset Grille take in the impressive rows of commercial, charter, and pleasure boats docked in West Ocean City, and the feel here is casual but well-heeled. Sunset Grille has three bars, indoor and outdoor seating, and live music in season. Their menu focuses, naturally, on seafood, and favorites include seared ahi tuna and fried tempura lobster. ($$$)

TEQUILA MOCKINGBIRD · moldy tortilla chips

(12919 Coastal Hwy ☎ *410.250.4424* ✎ *octequila.com)* This cantina, a favorite among locals, serves over 100 tequilas – they claim they have more than any other bar in Maryland – and a range of Mexican and domestic beers. The bonus is that while you're enjoying your Mexican refreshments, they'll serve you chunky, warm tortilla chips and chunky, spicy salsa. It's tempting to make a meal of just this, but you'd be missing out on some interesting entrees, including their Loco Polli, which is chicken breasts stuffed with lump crabmeat and chorizo, topped with chipotle cream sauce and cheddar cheese, then baked. Call for off-season hours. ($$)

WHISKERS PUB

(120th St. Bayside ☎ *410.524.2609* ⟨ *whiskerspub.com)* This noisy, friendly sports bar in North Ocean City is a favorite among locals, and a refuge for Redskins fans in a town that loves the Ravens. Well-used wooden bench booths, a long, comfortable bar, and plenty of sports trophies and memorabilia fill the long, narrow restaurant. Favorites here are burgers, French onion soup, and reuben sandwiches. They make great soup, so inquire about the soup of the day. ($$)

YANG'S PALACE

(5401 Coastal Hwy ☎ *410.723.4600)* None of the food here is great. But this might be just the place if you're with a big crowd and you've all had your fill of fried beach food and you can't all agree on what you want for dinner. Yang's is a large restaurant, and when you are seated you are given three menus: Chinese, Japanese, and Indian. In each case, the choices are fairly basic. The sushi is fresh but not particularly artful; the same can be said for the Indian and Chinese food. One nice surprise is the seaweed salad, which is crisp and fresh, sprinkled with crunchy sesame seeds, and generously proportioned. ($$)

FINE DINING

Ocean City's fine dining options have dramatically improved over the last several years. High-end restaurants including Galaxy 66, The Hobbit, Fager's Island Fine Dining, and Fausto's (with two locations) allow Ocean City vacationers to stay right in town when they have the urge to splurge on a fine meal. Many traditional Ocean City restaurants are still going strong, as well. Second and third generations of families plan special outings every year at Harrison's Harborwatch, Adolfo's, and the granddaddy of them all,

Phillips – or one of the other traditional seafood buffet restaurants that followed their lead.

ADOLFO'S

(806 S Baltimore Ave. ☎ *410.289.4001* ✆ *oc-adolfos.com)* Adolfo's is fine dining in the old Ocean City style, in a building that dates back to 1881 and survived the 1933 storm that created the inlet that can now be viewed from the restaurant's outdoor seating. The restaurant is an old-style Italian bistro, with house specials that include eggplant parmigiana and nightly surf and turf offerings. Their seafood bruschetta is excellent. ($$$)

FAGER'S ISLAND FINE DINING 🔲

(201 60th St. ☎ *410.524.5500* ✆ *fagers.com)* One of Ocean City's flagship fine dining restaurants, Fager's Island has a spectacular bayfront location and a confident, wide-ranging seasonal menu. Its dining room is comfortably sophisticated with a constellation of big paper lanterns softly lighting the room and jazzy world music providing a background to conversation. The Fager's Island wine list has been noted in *Wine Spectator* as the top wine list in Maryland. The list is so big, it has a table of contents and it changes as often as every few weeks as their cellar evolves. Over thirty-five wines are available by the glass at any given time. It's a pleasure to have wine pairings suggested by the staff, as they can do a better job of wading through the selections than all, but the most experienced wine connoisseur. The food menu is innovative without being absurd, and what comes out of the kitchen is excellent. The cooking is confident, the timing is perfect, and the presentation is simple and beautiful.

A recent menu included an appetizer of poblano peppers stuffed with chorizo, crabmeat, boursin cheese, and pancetta, with a pineapple salsa and a pepper sauce. It is a testament to the chef's talent that this concoction was sublime, and not ridiculous! Another surprising and delicious appetizer is the chicken livers wrapped in bacon along with water chestnuts. The prime rib is not to be missed: their specialty is to encrust the beef with garlic, black pepper and spices, and quickly sear it. As Ocean City evolves, more and more "upscale" dining is becoming available here. While new restaurants work hard (and some succeed) in creating an atmosphere of moneyed sophistication, Fager's Island Fine Dining feels comfortable and established. This makes dinner here feel relaxed rather than uptight.

A special menu is available that outlines common allergens, including gluten and nuts. ($$$)

FAUSTO'S ANTIPASTI [MUST SEE]

(11604 Coastal Hwy ☎ 410.723.3675 ⌂ ristoranteantipasti.com) Hunkered down behind one of North Ocean City's condo towers, Fausto's is in a low building that can't be seen from the street – and it's worth seeking out. It does have a sign out on Coastal Highway by the driveway, which helps. On their regular menu, the Timballo Di Mamma is not to be missed: thin sheets of homemade pasta layered with ground veal, Buffalo mozzarella and nutmeg for an unusual, rich supper. Or try one of their specials. Every day they make a different homemade pasta, soup, and entrée featuring the catch of the day.

Homemade tiramisu, cannoli and other traditional Italian desserts and expertly made espresso are a lovely ending to a meal here. Eat in the bar if you can. Its cozy red walls and candlelight are more comfortable than their white-tablecloth dining room. For the vacationer frazzled by too much mass-produced restaurant food, Fausto's will satisfy.

"We make everything. We try not to buy anything," their general manager said. "The difference in taste is phenomenal." This restaurant is one of three restaurants owned by Fausto DiCarlo, and its cozy setting and attention to detail make it the best of them. ($$$)

FRESCO'S FINE DINING

(82nd St. on the bay ☎ *410.524.8202* ✆ *ocfrescos.com)* The fact that "Fine Dining" is a part of Fresco's name sets off a little warning bell (unlike Fager's Island Fine Dining, which is so named to distinguish it from Fager's more casual bar and grill). Indeed, the pretensions exceed the execution at Fresco's. The décor is fussy and dated, while the prices are quite modern. That said, the menu has a few unusual and ambitious items on it, such as a Tuscan Fiocchi pasta entrée, which is pasta purses stuffed with mascarpone cheese and pears in a creamy sauce with roasted peppers and pine nuts, finished with Gorgonzola. Before dinner, visitors can have a drink at Fresco's nightclub, called the outdated name, Jive. ($$$)

GALAXY 66

(66th St. & Coastal Hwy ☎ *410.723.6762* ✆ *galaxy66barandgrille.com)* A fine example of the new, upscale side of Ocean City, this bayside restaurant and bar has an ambitious menu: one entrée is a filet mignon with a truffle demi-glaze, smashed potatoes with parmesan, and roasted asparagus. It's fun to get dressed up after a casual day at the beach and drink martinis at Galaxy 66's sparkly, black granite bar. The bright, primary colors and the upper deck seating are breezy and enjoyable, and it's easy to feel comfortable dressed up or down. The service is friendly and careful, though the dining room is quite loud and echoes. Check their web site for food and live music specials. ($$$)

HARRISON'S HARBOR WATCH

(806 S Boardwalk ☎ *410.289.5121)* This large restaurant sits at the very end of the Boardwalk, with a sweeping view of the inlet. The prices are high, the wait can be long, the staff (which is young and inexperienced) is slow and careless, and the food is good but not spectacular. The restaurant feels like a tourist trap, which is unfortunate, because its location is truly beautiful. ($$$)

THE HOBBIT

(121 81st St. ☎ *410.524.8100)* This elegant restaurant has shed much of its early Tolkien-themed decor at its third location. The previous location was demolished to make way for the condominium building, Rivendell, which now houses The Hobbit on its ground level. Some traditionalists miss the folksy charm of the little old house that was The Hobbit. However, the new dining room is truly lovely, and a fitting backdrop for the sophisticated food that comes out of the kitchen. Floor to ceiling windows face the bay right at water level, and the bay grasses are dramatically lit at night. This striking natural view is echoed by the grass-like branches that are lit against a soft green wall along the opposite side of the room.

Like other fine restaurants in Ocean City, The Hobbit is known for its excellent crab cakes. However, there are a couple of dishes here that are not available elsewhere, and worth trying. One is their Roast Prime, which is center cut and roasted rather than grilled, resulting in a meltingly tender piece of meat. Another is a dish of cashew-encrusted veal, which is rich and filling, and perfect for a rainy evening. A recent appetizer special was seared scallops with chilis and avocado, perfectly cooked and just spicy enough. Another special was a surprisingly simple, perfect salad with avocado and hearts of palm. The staff is friendly and attentive, and seems to understand that in a fine restaurant, the point is not to rush diners in and out as fast as possible. The Hobbit is a place to go and spend an evening savoring the food, the wine, and the soothing atmosphere. ($$$)

JULES

(11805 Coastal Hwy # N ☎ *410.524.3396* ◌ *julesoc.com)* Cool green walls and simple, sophisticated furnishings are just right for this North Ocean City gem, which sits in a bayside strip mall. The simple décor lets the food take center stage, and that's how it should be in this excellent fine dining restaurant. The menu focuses on seasonal and local foods, which means the menu always has several

outstanding seafood choices. Recent offerings included Chincoteague oysters on the half shell, and applewood-smoked, bacon-wrapped scallops with blackberry glaze, corn salsa, and adobo-tequila crème fraiche. The wine selection is also extensive, and staff is well-versed in food and wine pairings. This is a restaurant to keep in mind for special occasions and romantic evenings out. ($$$)

LIQUID ASSETS

(9301 Coastal Hwy ☎ 410.524.7037 ☎ ocliquidassets.com) The word is out about Liquid Assets, a longtime favorite of Ocean City locals. The restaurant used to be just a few tables and a bar perched in the center of a well-stocked liquor store. You could get the same food at Liquid Assets as they served in the high-end restaurant next door because the two places shared a kitchen. So you'd sit at a bistro table in the middle of a bunch of wine shipping cases and munch on utterly light, crunchy calamari, or seared scallop and mushroom risotto. Then the restaurant next door closed, and Liquid Assets knocked a hole in the wall and took over. They freshened up the front façade, and now Liquid Assets actually looks like a restaurant. You can still sit in the liquor store and eat, though, which is fun. The food is fresh, seasonal, and prepared with a light and practiced hand. And – no surprise – the wine list is extensive and the wait staff is knowledgeable about pairing wines with food. ($$$)

PHILLIP'S CRAB HOUSE

(2004 Philadelphia Ave. ☎ 410.289.6821 ⌂ phillipsseafood.com) This location has been an Ocean City fixture since 1956. It is the original location in a chain that now has other locations and franchises all over the East Coast, and it is still the choice for many families who want to have one big seafood dinner blowout while they're on vacation. The seafood buffet includes steamed whole crabs, crab legs, crab imperial, shrimp, fish, and other seafood choices, plus a beef carving station, fried chicken and several pasta choices. For

big eaters, this is the original Ocean City seafood buffet, and traditionalists swear by their annual Phillip's dinner. While Phillip's isn't the most modern or innovative restaurant in Ocean City, they have a niche that they fill with skill and care. This venerable original location doesn't seem to be resting on its laurels. ($$$)

RISTORANTE ANTIPASTI

(31st St. & Coastal Hwy ☎ 410.289.4588 ⚲ ristoranteantipasti.com) Ocean City has several really fine Italian restaurants, and Ristorante Antipasti, the flagship in a 3-restaurant chain, is one of them. The fact that this one is housed in a former Wendy's doesn't hurt anything! In fact, its warm brown walls and muted light are comfortable and sophisticated. Fresh fish specials are especially recommended. One daily special was a striped bass that was cooked in rock salt, filleted at the table, and finished with a drizzle of olive oil and freshly ground pepper. Ristorante Antipasti is known for its homemade pasta dishes and its authentic, light touch – no heavy tomato sauces or overpowering garlic flavors.

Owner and master chef Fausto DiCarlo was ruled a winner on the U.S. *Food Network* for his timballo Abrussese, a lasagna-like creation with thin pasta layers covering ground veal, buffalo mozzarella and nutmeg filling. The result is gentle and less filling than lasagna. This award allows Ristorante Antipasti to include on its sign the words, "Top Five in the Country FAUSTO." Sometimes Fausto himself offers cooking classes; call the restaurant for details. ($$$)

THE SHARK ON THE HARBOR

(12924 Sunset Ave. on the commercial fishing harbor ☎ 410.213.0924 ⚲ ocshark.com) Another good steak and seafood restaurant over in West Ocean City, The Shark has a policy of using organic produce, grains and dairy products, antibiotic-free meat and wild-caught seafood. A signature entrée is grilled tenderloin filet of natural beef topped with a walnut & bleu cheese pate and caramelized Granny

Smith apples and red onions, accompanied by lobster mashed potatoes. ($$$)

TUTTI GUSTI

(3322 Coastal Hwy ☎ *410.289.3318* ✆ *tutti-gusti.com)* Dinner will put a big dent in your wallet, but that's to be expected for really fine food in Ocean City (and sometimes, for not-so-great food in Ocean City.) Tutti Gusti specializes in northern Italian fare, and always has over a dozen daily specials. All of their food is made from scratch, from bread to mozzarella to pasta to dessert. Even their fish comes in whole and is butchered on-site. There is an emphasis on fresh seafood dishes with a light Italian preparation. ($$$)

Nightlife

The trend in Ocean City nightlife over the past several years has been towards big, bayside island-themed or bar and grill-style restaurants with big, comfortable music venues incorporated right in.

Much of Ocean City's nightlife happens right in its restaurants. Most dinner places, bayside or not, have a bar of some sort incorporated into the restaurant. Many fun evenings can be spent visiting and sipping cocktails just a few steps away from the dinner table after a satisfying restaurant meal.

Then there's the more traditional downtown Ocean City bar scene, which still thrives on summer nights. Finally, there are a number of watering holes around town that don't really fit either category, but deserve a nod.

BAYSIDE NIGHTLIFE

Bayside nightlife is crowded fun. Bayside restaurants that are also fun indoor/outdoor nightspots are **Castaways** *(105 64th St.* ☎ *410-524-9090 ⌀ castawaysoc.com)*, **Fish Tales** *(22nd St. and the bay* ☎ *410.289.7438 ⌀ ocfishtales.com)*, **Macky's Bayside Bar & Grill** *(5311 Coastal Hwy* ☎ *410.723.5565 ⌀ mackys.com)*, **M.R. Ducks** *(Talbot St. and the bay* ☎ *800.659.7703 ⌀ talbotstreetpier.com/mrducks)*, **Harpoon Hanna's** *(Rt. 54 and the bay* ☎ *302.539.3095)*, and the string of bars and restaurants along the commercial harbor in West Ocean City.

SEACRETS

(49th St. & the bay ☎ *410.524.4900 ⌀ seacrets.com)* This place does a great job with both food and nightlife and is definitely the biggest party in town that starts around lunchtime. The Jamaican-themed bayside compound floats big rafts in the water on summer days, and patrons can enjoy cocktails right in the bay. They offer indoor

and outdoor seating, and up to five bands or DJs play at any one time. Usually the music includes a cover band or locally popular rock or hip-hop band, and some reggae or ska. Nationally-known acts occasionally play here too. Seacrets also runs its own independent radio station (98.1, Ocean 98, or Irieradio). The line between indoors and outdoors blurs at Seacrets, with its sandy floors and thickets of palm trees. The crowd is generally young, but Seacrets is so large and popular that there are always plenty of people in their 30s, 40s, and 50s there too. There is often a line of cars, including a limousine or two, waiting to drop passengers at the front entrance. The sight of this, along with the Seacrets radio antenna rising as a light-spangled beacon into the night sky, creates the kind of visual buzz that is unmatched anywhere else in town.

FAGER'S ISLAND

(201 60th St. ☎ *410.524.5500* ✎ *fagers.com)* This establishment is another big party on summer afternoons and evenings in Ocean City. A longstanding favorite of locals and vacationers, Fager's Island hosts a cheerful sunset party every afternoon on its multi-level deck, pier, and gazebo. The 1812 Overture is timed to play each day so that the cannons fire just as the sun hits the waterline. The crowd inevitably breaks into applause for another gorgeous day at the beach. If you sit at the bar, expect your bartender to introduce himself and shake your hand. The menu is full of snacks, sandwiches, and light fare. Fager's is the most popular night spot for a slightly older crowd than Seacrets.

THE BOARDWALK AND DOWNTOWN

It's illegal to carry an open alcoholic beverage on the Boardwalk itself, but a grand time can be had making stops at the many bars up and down the boards. Start at the Inlet Bar all the way down at the end of the Boardwalk by the Lifesaving Museum—the sign just says "Bar". This is old school Ocean City: wood paneling, plenty of neon beer signs and mirrors, a couple of still-functioning pinball machines in the back, and a bartender who is friendly but hasn't cracked open a can of Polite Customer Service. There's no band, plenty of old rock music on the jukebox, and if you're hungry, you can go next door to the connecting sandwich shop and soda fountain.

From here, it's an easy stroll down the Boardwalk to a group of bars around Wicomico Street that cater to the biker crowd but are fun for any unpretentious, fun-loving tourist: The Bearded Clam *(15 Wicomico St.* ☎ *410.289.4498* ✋ *thebeardedclam.com)*, The Cork Bar *(3 Wicomico St.* ☎ *410.289.6921),* Snapper's Saloon *(501 S Baltimore Ave.* ☎ *410.289.3073* ✋ *coldbeer.com).*

If you're looking for live music downtown, you'll find several Boardwalk bars are longstanding venues for live music.

THE PURPLE MOOSE

(108 S Boardwalk ☎ *410.289.6953* ✋ *purplemoosesaloon.com)* This establishment is home to big, fun, loud rock music. Live bands play nightly, and there's usually a cover charge. You'll find a mix of rock cover bands and local favorites here, and generally an older crowd than is found at the other big live music venues in town.

SHENANIGANS

(4th St. & the Boardwalk ☎ *410.289.7181* ✋ *ocshenanigans.com)* This bar has an Irish-themed menu of casual food to accompany its Irish beers and drink specials, and hosts live Irish music many nights in-season.

BRASS BALLS

(1105 Boardwalk ☎ *410.289.0069* ✋ *brassballssaloon.com)* A vintage fringy lamp and dark wood kind of saloon, Brass Balls also features live music, deejays, and karaoke in season.

PEPPERS TAVERN 🆚

(Basement at 16ᵗʰ St. & the Boardwalk ☎ *410.289.8444* ⌂ *5stardive.com)* A gleefully divey Mexican restaurant and cantina with a mix-your-own Bloody Mary bar and nachos "as big as your head", their shop also sells hundreds of hot sauces and Bloody Mary mixes, and their guacamole is the best in Ocean City.

MORE NIGHTLIFE

Ocean City nightlife extends up and down Coastal Highway in season (some would say the best party is actually on the bus that travels from one end to the other!) Here are a few places other than the Boardwalk bars and the bayside clubs that might just suit your tastes perfectly.

THE PARTY BLOCK

(17th and Coastal Highway ☎ *410.289.6331* ⌂ *partyblock.com)* The Party Block is a complex of three night clubs catering to young twenty-somethings – and those who still feel like young twenty-somethings. It consists of **The Big Kahuna**, **Paddock**, and **Rush**, as well as a large **Pool Bar**. The Paddock is a live music venue that hosts rock and hip-hop acts. The Big Kahuna is, of course, a Hawaiian surf-themed club, and at Rush, the bartenders wear lingerie. At prices starting at $150, partiers can rent a poolside cabana or daybed, which comes with a pitcher of sangrias or mojitos, or a bottle of premium liquor and mixers. Galaxy 66 provides the food for the Pool Bar's cabana menu. The crowd is young and striving to be sophisticated, and the prices reflect this same grasping attitude.

BUXY'S SALTY DOG

(28th St. & Coastal Hwy ☎ *410.289.0973* ⌂ *buxyssaltydog.com)* This place is on the other end of the spectrum with its paws in the sand,

but its heart back in Pittsburgh. Every sports event is a good enough reason for celebration at the Salty Dog, and that is especially true when the Steelers are playing. This is a comfortable pub with casual food and daily specials.

JOHNNY B'S COWBOYZ SMOKEHOUSE & SALOON

(Above Gold Coast Mall, 114th St. ☝ cowboyzsaloon.com) If your tastes lean more towards country music, try Johnny B's. By day, Johnny B's is a great place to get a big ol' burger or brisket sandwich and kick back at one of the bars, either indoors or out. If there's a game on, this is the place to go to see it on multiple giant screens. At night, the ten-gallon hats come out on the large dance floor, with country and western line dancing. Johnny B's can be tricky to find: it's on the 2nd floor of the Gold Coast Mall, up a long, dark flight of stairs at the back.

H20

(Worcester St. & Baltimore Ave. ☎ *410.289.7102)* Kids under 21 have their own nightclub in Ocean City. This large dance club is open to ages fifteen to twenty every night in season, with a different theme each night.

Accommodations

Ocean City has the plushest accommodations any traveler could want, as well as the most basic. Over eight million people visit Ocean City annually, and they stay at the hundreds and hundreds of hotels, motels, rental condos, and campsites available.

Young people who are more interested in being close to the noise and fun of the Boardwalk will want to stay in the southern end of town, from the inlet to about 6th Street. Ocean City history buffs and die-hard traditionalists will also want to stay close to the inlet, perhaps in one of the historic Boardwalk hotels.

Families looking for a little bit of peace and quiet with convenient access to downtown fun will want to stay anywhere from around 10th Street all the way up to about 60th Street. There are many, many places to stay in this midtown area, both on the ocean side and bayside. When Ocean City was expanding northwards in the 1950s and '60s, "modern" motor court motels sprung up from around 15th Street to 33rd Street, and many of these still exist.

Those who want quick access to more of the high-end restaurants and perhaps wish to stay in a high-rise tower with a sweeping view will prefer a North Ocean City hotel or condo rental. The traffic is less snarled, and the evenings are quieter here, though you'll find hustle and bustle during the summer season wherever you go in Ocean City.

Another category to consider is a bayside hotel or rental condo. The sunsets over the bay are breathtaking and the pace is slower. Plus, those who wish to get out on the water in a rental boat or Jet Ski might find the bayside to be more convenient and more fun.

There are notable exceptions to each of these guidelines, but this should help you distinguish among the different parts of town.

During the month of June, Ocean City is the vacation destination for thousands of graduating high school students experiencing their first taste of freedom. A number of hotels cater to these students. A list can be found online *(⊕ ococean.com/play.html)*, under the student accommodations link. This is also, frankly, a good list to check if you want to avoid the places where these students, known to the locals as "Junebugs," often stay.

Another thing to decide is whether you'd like to stay in a hotel, rent a condo, or camp. If you'd like the ease and service of a hotel, you can choose from literally hundreds – from four-star boutique hotels to bargain basics. While advance reservations are always a good idea, with hotel stays there is a bit more opportunity to be spontaneous and stay an extra day than with condo rentals.

For families staying more than a couple of nights, renting a condo is probably a less expensive and more comfortable option, since there is a fully equipped kitchen for making money-saving meals. Staying in a rental apartment or a condo means bringing your own bed and bath linens and paper supplies. Kitchens are equipped for cooking, and beds have pillows and blankets. Condos often feel more like home (because they are somebody's vacation home), and have a bit more living space than hotel rooms.

A dizzying list of Ocean City condo rental services can be found online *(⊕ atbeach.com/rental.html)*. However, the single most extensive listing of Ocean City condo rental properties is at **Coldwell Banker** *(☎ 800.633.1000 ⊕ cbvacations.com)*. If their web site has too much to choose from (it includes over 4,500 properties), you can then call them as well. The rental agents you speak to are actually in Ocean City, and are very familiar with the territory.

Camping is also a great way to experience the seashore. Camping at Assateague Island is discussed separately in the chapter on Assateague. However, there are other camping options around Ocean City covered in this section.

Many hotels close up for the winter season; those that stay open offer great off-season rates. For a terrific winter getaway, give your favorite hotel a call and see if they are offering any specials. Even in the summer season, rates vary from week to week, with the most expensive time to go being mid to late July. Also, weekday hotel stays are cheaper than weekends. Many rental condos are only offered by the week. If you're able to visit in May or September, you'll find cheaper accommodations, beautiful weather, and fewer crowds.

Price ranges are given for the summer season and are indicated as follows: *$ = less than $150 per night, $$ = $150-$250 per night, $$$ = more than $250 per night.* Remember, when you are considering prices, to take into account that some apartments and condominiums sleep large groups, making what sounds like a steep price tag more affordable if you're traveling with several other people.

INLET/DOWNTOWN AREA

There are many bargain-priced choices for students looking for a place to lay their heads at night. This site *(⌀ ococean.com/play.html)* lists all the hotels catering to these visitors. Many of the hotels included on the student list are in the inlet/downtown area. The hotels listed here are all located directly on the Boardwalk, and some have interesting historical significance.

CORONET APARTMENTS
(1215 Boardwalk ☎ *410.289.6305* ⌀ *vrbo.com/124804)* This old-fashioned brown-shingled building has a deck that connects with the Boardwalk, and Adirondacks for relaxing and watching the beach crowd go by. The winner of a Beauty Spot award given by the town of Ocean City to the town's most beautiful properties, this establishment offers large four-bedroom apartments that are available by the week. Like most vacation apartment rentals, kitchens are fully equipped, and renters need to bring only linens and paper supplies. ($$$)

HAMPTON HOUSE/LAMBROS APARTMENTS

(Bdwk & 4th St ☎ 800.564.7582 ⏁ ocean-city.com/lambrosandhampton)
This property is a small, old-fashioned Boardwalk hotel with
rooms, efficiencies, and apartments for rent. Two levels of porches
with awnings and plenty of chairs for lounging make this a comfortable choice for staying right in the middle of everything, downtown. The hotel-provided parking alone is a valuable commodity in
this neighborhood. ($$)

HARRISON HALL

(Boardwalk at 15th St. ☎ 800.638.2106) Large, brown pillars two
stories tall hold up the roof on the beachside porch of this stately
old hotel, open for nearly 60 years. While the hotel is not particu-
larly modern, it is clean and serviceable, and its prices are quite rea-
sonable considering its perfect location. The Adirondacks on the
porch afford a beautiful view of the Boardwalk and the beach. ($)

INN ON THE OCEAN

(1001 Boardwalk ☎ 410.289.8894 ⏁ innontheocean.com) This small,
private home is the only bed and breakfast on the Boardwalk, and
it's charming. Its blue-striped awnings and white wicker porch fur-
niture are the very picture of gracious east coast beach living. The
inn's porch and deck open right onto a relatively quieter part of the
Boardwalk. The formal dining room and sitting room are furnished
with fine antiques and fresh flowers, and the feel here is elegant
without being fussy. The B&B has six rooms available for adults,
with either queen or king beds. Some have Jacuzzis, and the
Oceana Room has its own private balcony overlooking the ocean.
The owner is known for her lavish breakfasts, and some of her
recipes can be found on the inn's web site. ($$$)

THE LANKFORD HOTEL

(807 Boardwalk ☎ *800.282.9709* ⌂ *lankfordhotel.com)* This Ocean City landmark is the oldest wooden hotel on the beach. It was established in 1924 by Mary Quillen, who named it after her aunt Amelia Coffin Lankford. It still looks much as it did when it first opened, with a wide, handsome porch and a comfortable jumble of Victorian furniture in the lobby. The Lankford has become a destination for stitching guilds. These groups, including the Delaware Valley Historical Samplers Guild, book-stitching weekends here because of the presence of an excellent stitchery shop, **Salty Yarns** *(⌂ saltyyarns.com)* on the ground floor of the hotel. During stitching weekends, participants sit in the lobby with its impressive ocean view and work on their projects with the aid of bright lighting that has been placed throughout the room for this purpose. The hotel has no elevator, and the rooms are small, but clean and quaintly furnished with period furnishings. All rooms have private baths, air conditioning, phones, and cable—so it's not a complete time warp. Rich, deep paint colors are used throughout the hotel, as they were when it was first built. ($)

THE MAJESTIC

(Boardwalk at 7th St. ☎ *410.289.6262* ⌂ *ocmajestichotel.com)* Originally called Liberty Farms Hotel but renamed in 1945, the Majestic is one of the many hotels that used to offer "the American plan," which included meals along with room rental. The Majestic was once known for its sticky buns and oyster pies. Those days are gone, but the Majestic is still a family-owned hotel with wicker rockers on the large porches and guests who return every year. The rooms offer basic amenities, and the outdoor pool is heated, which is great on blustery days early in the season. This is one of the few tastes of traditional Ocean City life left standing on the Boardwalk. ($)

MARTY'S PLAYLAND APARTMENTS

(5 Worcester St. ☎ *410.289.7271* ⊕ *martysplayland.com/products.htm)* If your absolute favorite thing in Ocean City is the inlet end of the Boardwalk – the Ground Zero of arcades and carnival rides – then Marty's Playland Apartments might be just your cup of tea. These rental units are mostly on the 2nd and 3rd floor over Marty's Playland arcade. So guests can roll out of bed and report directly to the Boardwalk rides and games each day. The units are simply furnished and clean. Pack your earplugs if you want to get any sleep! ($$)

PLIM PLAZA

(Boardwalk & 2nd St. ☎ *800.837.3587* ⊕ *plimplazaoc.com)* This large hotel right in the heart of the busy Boardwalk is all that's left of one of Ocean City's original hotels, The Plimhimmon. Other than the rocking chairs on the veranda facing the Boardwalk, there are not many reminders of the original hotel here. The 181 single rooms have a great downtown location, but they are neither freshly renovated nor quaintly old-fashioned. A Caribbean-themed pool bar with multiple jacuzzis sways to live music during the season, and a macaw named Dakota keeps an eye on the lobby. Open April through October. ($$)

MIDTOWN

Mid-town is the right choice for people looking for convenience to both the fun of downtown and the plentiful dining, shopping, and mini-golfing found in the more northern part of town. Also, the Convention Center sits at 40th Street and Coastal Highway, making many mid-town accommodations quite convenient for convention-goers. Remember: the Boardwalk ends at 27th Street, and the north end of the Boardwalk is relatively quiet. Beyond the Boardwalk, of course, there is no bike or trolley traffic—only sand dunes—between oceanfront buildings and the sand.

BAHIA MAR AND SURFSIDE COTTAGES

(6 & 8 43rd St. ☎ *571.436.2844* ✆ *bahiamaroceancity.com)* This small compound of family-owned weekly rental units are meticulously maintained, and just a few steps from the sand. They're great for families with children, and their fully equipped kitchens are modern and clean. The location is convenient to the Convention Center and Seacrets, with a small grocery store just across Coastal Highway, a great crab place right around the corner, and a bus stop at the end of the block. Open seasonally. ($$)

CASTLE IN THE SAND

(3701 Atlantic Ave. ☎ *800.552.SAND* ✆ *castleinthesand.com)* The proprietors of this sprawling hotel complex clearly have fun with their castle motif. Royal crests and statues of knights and kings are liberally sprinkled throughout the buildings and grounds, and the hotel's Olympic-sized swimming pool is the largest in Ocean City. Its Coconuts Bar and Grill offers live local entertainment beachside during the summer season, and its sand volleyball courts are often busy—sometimes with school volleyball teams who stay here when they're in town for tournaments. The hotel has weekly cottage rentals, and oceanfront rooms. The rooms themselves are clean and serviceable, but not luxurious. ($$)

COCONUT MALORIE

(200 59th St. on the bay ☎ *800.767.6060* ✆ *coconutmalorie.com)* A 5-story hotel on the bayfront, Coconut Malorie has eighty-five upscale suites with custom-designed furniture, private balconies with lovely bay views, marble bathrooms with Jacuzzi tubs, full kitchens with granite countertops, an outdoor heated pool, and laundry facilities on each floor. Its grandiose lobby has a curving, white marble staircase befitting a princess, but a bit frightening for a mere

mortal wearing tiny, strappy sandals. The hotel has confer-
ence/event facilities for up to 200. A lighted footbridge connects
the Coconut Malorie with the excellent Fager's Island Restaurant.
($$$)

COLLINWOOD APARTMENTS [MUST SEE]

(12 34th St. ☎ *410.251.6150* ⏚ *collinwoodcottages.com)* Collinwood
Apartments is a collection of five small beach cottages, built by the
Collins family in the 1950s and 1960s. Fortunately, it has main-
tained what looks to be pretty much their original condition ever
since. The owners guess that these are probably the last ocean cot-
tage rentals available in Ocean City, which used to be chock full of
them. The little buildings are clean and trim, freshly painted and
simply furnished. Rather than being oriented towards the street, the
cottages face in towards a couple of central gathering spots. An
outdoor kitchen is the social center of the cottages; there are also
hammocks and quiet spots to hang out under the shade of a tree or
an umbrella. The cottages have been operated by the family as va-
cation rental units since their inception, and most rentals are
monthly or seasonal, and by referral only. However, weekly rentals
do occasionally open up, and it's definitely worth a phone call to
see if there's a vacancy. Open seasonally. ($$)

DAYS INN OCEANFRONT

(2200 Baltimore Ave. ☎ *800.926.1122* ⏚ *daysinnboardwalk.com)* This
mid-priced hotel has an extensive garden, with flowers, pergolas,
and fountains surrounding the property. One of the Days Inn's two
buildings is called the French Quarter because of its lacy wrought-
iron architectural decorations. The amenities in the French Quarter
building and the other building, which is oceanfront, are compara-
ble; the rooms are fairly clean and serviceable but could use some
updating. The exception to this is the 4th and 5th floor of the
oceanfront building. These floors have been completely renovated
into studios, with upgraded kitchens and bathrooms, and large

floor plans that include two double beds plus a living room area with a large balcony overlooking the Boardwalk and the ocean. Guests receive discounted tickets to the Jolly Rogers amusement park, which is just across Coastal Highway. The hotel complex includes an outdoor pool, restaurant, pub, pool bar, and a banquet room with an attached kitchen for family reunions or business functions. Open April through mid-October. ($$)

DUNES MANOR

(2800 Baltimore Ave. ☎ *800.523.2888* ⌂ *dunesmanor.com)* Dunes Manor is a very large oceanfront hotel with all the modern amenities, but its Victorian hospitality is reminiscent of the old days of Ocean City. A simple but elegant complimentary afternoon tea with scones and clotted cream is served daily in the lobby, which has ample comfortable seating and a grand piano. Guests linger and visit with one another at tea much like they might have 100 years ago, rather than retreating to their own rooms. Every evening the hotel provides piano music in this same setting. The lobby level also has a balcony all the way across the ocean side of the building, with rocking chairs and a beautiful beachfront view. Also in the hotel are the Victorian Room restaurant, which serves breakfast, lunch, and dinner; and the Zippy Lewis Lounge, a small and clubby bar named after a legendary early Ocean City character. The rooms are clean and serviceable, and include either two double or two king-sized beds; all rooms have microwaves, little fridges, and coffeemakers. Every room also has an oceanfront balcony. The rooms are nothing special (except for that grand balcony view), but that's not the point. It is the warmth of the hospitality downstairs that draws guests to stay. The hotel can host group events in its ballroom. ($$)

THE EDGE AT FAGER'S ISLAND

(60th St. at the Bay ☎ *888.371.5400* ⌂ *fagers.com/edge)* Built at the bay's edge in 2002, The Edge was the first "designer hotel" in

Maryland. Larry Peabody, an important mid-century furniture and interior designer who created the design for several hotels in the United States and the Caribbean, traveled the world with owner John Fager to select furniture for each of the themed rooms. With just twelve rooms overlooking the bay and a small pool with poolside beverage service, guest can choose to stay in such whimsically named rooms as "Bliss", "Michelle" (French Provincial-inspired), "Safari", and "Hang Five" (with a redwood tub surround and a surfboard propped against the wall). In every case, rooms include sumptuously elegant bathrooms (each with different styles of ceramic or natural stone tile and walk-in showers), double Jacuzzi tubs, gas or electric fireplaces, and sumptuous bed linens that include down comforters. Two rooms at The Edge are suites, which is great except that the Jacuzzi bath still sits prominently in the main room. So if two couples stay in a suite, the tub is not a particularly useful amenity unless the four traveling partners are, shall we say, unusually close. ($$$)

THE EMPRESS MOTEL
(20th St. & Baltimore Ave. ☎ *800.406.8060* ⌁ *empressmotel.com)* This motel is still owned and managed by the same family who built it, and the attention to detail and cleanliness is evident. Though not oceanfront, The Empress is on the ocean side of Baltimore Avenue, so guests don't have to cross the busy street to get to the sand. When you call to make reservations, you may well speak to the owner herself. This is a no-nonsense, well-run, budget-friendly motel. ($)

THE FLAMINGO MOTEL
(3100 Baltimore Ave. ☎ *800.394.7465* ⌁ *flamingo-ocmd.com)* The Flamingo is one of Ocean City's motel row classics, with its snazzy pink neon sign and pink-trimmed balconies. The motel has three buildings, the first of which dates back to 1963. Guests can choose from single rooms, efficiencies, kitchenettes, and suites. The motel

has an indoor and outdoor pool, and a prime oceanfront location. Open March through October. ($$)

HILTON SUITES OCEAN CITY OCEANFRONT

(3200 Baltimore Ave. ☎ *866.729.3200* 🖰 *oceancityhilton.com)* Easily the most luxurious family-friendly hotel in Ocean City, the 4-star Hilton offers all oceanfront suites in a large mid-town hotel that's open year-round. The hotel, which opened in 2006, has an indoor pool and two outdoor pools with sweeping Atlantic Ocean views. One outdoor pool is for the adults, with a swim-up bar. The other is for children, with slides, fountains, and a mid-pool sunken pirate ship. 32 Palms, their elegant but understated fine dining restaurant, feels muted and starched without being particularly glamorous—an unfortunate combination in this town that thrives on a mix of complete informality and over-the-top glitziness. However, the high-end room amenities (Jacuzzi tubs, kitchens with full-size appliances and granite countertops, plasma-screen TVs, fine bed linens and lovely beach views) make this the finest oceanfront hotel in Ocean City. ($$$)

THE LIGHTHOUSE AT FAGER'S ISLAND

(60th St. at the bay ☎ *888.371.5400* 🖰 *fagers.com/hotel)* Those who prefer luxury accommodations that feel comfortable and seasoned rather than sharp and modern will find that The Lighthouse is the finest hotel in Ocean City. Along with The Edge at Fager's Island and the Hilton, this is one of the only 4-star hotels in town. It is easy to see why. The hotel's octagonal, red-roofed design was inspired by the Thomas Point Lighthouse in the Chesapeake Bay. Each room has a balcony overlooking either the open bay or bay wetlands, which teem with blue herons and other scenic sea birds. All of the rooms are furnished with pieces created by designer Larry Peabody specifically for the hotel, so the scale and the space in each room feels perfect. Peabody created honey-colored pieces that look like they're wrapped in lengths of bamboo. Upholstery,

exquisite bed linens, and towels are all in snowy white. Bathrooms
are elegantly simple, tiled from floor to ceiling in squares of white
marble. Each room has a cozy gas fireplace, a flat-screen TV, and
three phones. The hotel provides olive-oil based soaps and spa
robes, plus a nice packet of bath salts that are perfect for a soak in
the two-person Jacuzzi. This is tucked under the eaves and surrounded with mirrors and white marble. The kitchenette is stocked
with complimentary sodas and water, and a fresh pair of breakfast
pastries baked by the Fager's Island pastry chef. On the lower level
of the hotel is a lounge with French doors that open onto a covered deck with rocking chairs and a direct, sweeping view of the
bay. The lounge also has a fireplace and several comfortable seating
areas, as well as a bar with complimentary coffee and freshly baked
cookies each afternoon. An honor bar is also set up with a selection
of beer and wine. The scale of the whole hotel is small and inti-
mate, and feels European both in style and in its careful but comfortable service. Along with the Edge, this is the very best place in
Ocean City for a couple's getaway. ($$$)

QUALITY INN
(3301 Atlantic Ave ☎ *410.289.1234* ⏚ *qualityinnandsuitesoceancity.com)*
A mid-priced, mid-town hotel with both suites and efficiencies, the
Quality Inn is right across Coastal Highway from the Jolly Roger
Amusement Park, making it a popular choice for many families.
With indoor and outdoor pools and select rooms with Jacuzzi tubs,
this is a more affordable choice for families spending their summer
vacation at the beach, or business people in town for events at the
nearby convention center. The room furnishings are clean but a bit
dated. The views from the big balconies, though, never go out of
fashion. Open year round. ($$)

STOWAWAY GRAND
(2100 Baltimore Ave. ☎ *800.447.6779* ⏚ *grandhoteloceancity.com)* A
circle of cherubs frolicking in a fountain greets guests at the en-

trance to the Gateway Grand Hotel, a very large, semi-circular hotel with hotel room views that are either ocean front or ocean and bay view, depending on where along the half-moon shape of the hotel your room is located. On the 6th floor there is a restaurant and lounge with an impressive view of the bay, plus the usual array of upscale hotel amenities: indoor and outdoor pools, sauna, fitness center, and game room. The restaurant, coffee shop, salon, and lobby-level shops are not owned by the hotel but are tenants, and there is a slightly disjointed feel to the place as a result. There is no room service at the hotel because of this arrangement. Nevertheless, the hotel is consistently booked even through the shoulder seasons because of its impressive ballroom and banquet facilities. ($$)

THUNDERBIRD MOTEL

(Ocean @ 32 St ☎ 800.638.3244 ⌂ purnellproperties.com/thunderbird) At the Thunderbird you can get a wood-paneled room with a couple of double beds and a parking spot right out front. It's a bit threadbare, and there's no lazy river or sunken pirate ship in the motel's outdoor swimming pool. However, the Thunderbird is affordable, and has a location every bit as stellar as the Hilton, which is right next door. Open March through September. ($)

UPTOWN

There are a few good hotel choices in North Ocean City, but there is an enormous selection of rental condos in this part of town, as this is where the high-rise condominium buildings are located. This website *(⌂ oc-condos.com)* is a good single resource for information about high-rise condo rentals. In some cases, a single building will have some units renting as hotel rooms, while others are actually condominiums. The Carousel is one example of this multi-use situation. Whether the unit you rent is a condo rental or a hotel rental will make no difference, though, when you check in and use the property's services.

BONITA BEACH HOTEL
(8100 Coastal Hwy ☎ *410.520.0400* ⌂ *bonitabeachhotel.com)* This newer property has some of the amenities of the really upscale hotels in town, at a surprisingly affordable price. Their indoor swimming pool and fitness room are clean and modern, and the furnishings in the efficiency rooms are surprisingly inviting, with warm colors and plush upholstered furnishings. The hotel is not oceanfront, but it is on the beach side of Coastal Highway, and its uptown location puts it near some of Ocean City's best restaurants. No food service is available at the Bonita Beach Hotel. ($$)

THE CAROUSEL
(11700 Coastal Hwy ☎ *800.641.0011* ⌂ *Carouselhotel.com)* The Carousel was the hotel that ushered in the upscale, uptown Ocean City of the 1960s. To walk into the lobby now, with its slightly cramped, slightly tired décor, is a bit of a letdown. That said, there's no getting around the fact that there is an ice skating rink in the hotel's atrium. It's true! It's really fun to come in from a hot day on the beach and go for a spin around the ice. Otherwise, you can find better pools, more upscale hotel rooms, and more updated décor elsewhere, often for less money. ($$)

FENWICK INN
(13801 Coastal Hwy ☎ *800.492.1873* ⌂ *fenwickinn.com)* Fenwick Inn has been a fixture at the top end of Ocean City for years, yet the rooms look fresh and modern. Jordan's Rooftop Restaurant is another draw, with its sweeping ocean and bay views, and live entertainment with some of the classic Rock and Roll greats, including Chubby Checkers and the Platters. You can call the restaurant (☎ *410.250.1867)* for music information. Fenwick Inn also has a large, recently updated indoor pool and Jacuzzi. ($$)

THE SEA HAWK MOTEL

(12410 Coastal Hwy ☎ *800.942.9042* ✆ *seahawkmotel.com)* It is likely that you will be greeted personally by the owner of The Sea Hawk when you arrive at this North Ocean City motel. The Sea Hawk is located on the ocean side of the highway, and near to Ocean City's beautiful Northside Park. The motel's turquoise and white paint and its turquoise beach umbrellas around the pool make for a classic old-fashioned motel atmosphere. Rooms are basic and clean. ($$)

WEST OCEAN CITY

There are few options for accommodations in West Ocean City, though more condo rentals are becoming available as this part of town experiences a building boom. There is shuttle service from the West Ocean City Park and Ride *(12848 Ocean Gateway* ✆ *ococean.com/park&ride.html)* to the South Division Street Transit Center at the inlet in downtown Ocean City. However, you'll want to drive to the Park and Ride lot rather than walk, as Ocean Gateway is not pedestrian friendly.

THE ALAMO MOTEL

(12614 Ocean Gateway ☎ *410.213.1884* ✆ *atbeach.com/lodging/alamo)* If you want a taste of Old Mexico on the Eastern Shore, The Alamo is just perfect. Though, think about it for a minute. Do you really want to sleep in this gleefully ramshackle, tumbledown motor lodge on the highway outside of Ocean City? The rooms are dark and smell stale, and the walls that look like stucco on the outside reveal themselves to be plain old concrete blocks when viewed from inside the hotel rooms. Honestly, if you're curious about this funky Tex-Mex themed motor lodge, just spend an evening drink-

ing Mexican beer at the restaurant and pool bar, and get it out of
your system. ($)

FRANCIS SCOTT KEY FAMILY RESORT

(12806 Ocean Gateway ☎ *410.213.0088* ✆ *Fskfamily.com)* The Francis Scott Key Family Resort is the very picture of a well-run, kid-
friendly, affordable family motel – with a bunch of extras. Kids will
absolutely love it. Without even leaving the grounds, they can play
in a big, fun indoor pool with buckets of water that splash down
from overhead, a spouting whale, and water slide. This is in addition to two outdoor swimming pools, playgrounds, a picnic pavilion that's great for family reunions, complimentary board game and
DVD rentals, and a shuttle service that runs on a regular basis from
the resort's front door to the Boardwalk at the inlet. The Francis
Scott Key also has a popular restaurant, the Marlin Moon Grill,
which has won awards from Wine Spectator and the Maryland Restaurant Association. It's a stretch to consider staying off the island
when visiting Ocean City, but families with active young children
should consider the Francis Scott Key. ($)

CAMPING

The most famous place for camping near Ocean City is Assateague,
which is covered elsewhere in this book. There are some other options, though, whether you are a tent camper or travel in an RV.

CASTAWAYS RV RESORT AND CAMPGROUND

(15550 Eagles Nest Rd. ☎ *410.213.0097* ✆ *castawaysrvoc.com)* Next
door to the award-winning Eagles Landing Golf Course, Castaways
is growing from a simple campground to a full-blown camping resort, with its own sand beach on the Sinepuxent Bay, beachside and
inland rental cabins, two swimming pools, piers for fishing and
crabbing, and for docking your boat. A new lodge with a store,

fitness facilities, TV lounge and wi-fi is planned. This is the closest campground to Ocean City, and also the most fun and island-funky. Open and wooded campsites are available, as are rental kayaks and jetskis, and fishing bait and tackle. Brightly painted school buses serve as courtesy beach shuttles. The campground is very dog friendly, and includes a separate Dog Beach. As with any good campground, there is a cheerful, relaxed attitude at Castaways, and it's tempting to pitch a tent here and not even bother going into town. ($)

FORT WHALEY CAMPGROUND

(11224 Dale Rd. ☎ *888.322.7717* ⏏ *fortwhaley.com/fortwhaley.cfm)* The quiet cousin to Frontier Town Family Campground, Fort Whaley is located about fifteen minutes west of Ocean City, right on Route 50. That's great if you're tired from driving and just want to pitch a tent and be done with it. However, it's not an especially picturesque location. If you're looking for Wild West-themed camping, Frontier Town's campground is the better bet. Fort Whaley's bathhouses are clean and well maintained, and camping is available under the trees and out in the open. In a less action-packed vacation destination than Ocean City, Fort Whaley's activities and amenities – including a catch and release fishing pond, a game room with pool tables, and arts and crafts shop – would be just fine. With Ocean City right down the highway, though, these amenities are not enough to make a discerning tourist stick around. Fortunately, Fort Whaley runs a shuttle into Ocean City from the campground. Guests get free admission to Frontier Town Water Park, and a 20% discount to the Frontier Town Western Theme Park. ($)

FRONTIER TOWN FAMILY CAMPGROUND

(8428 Stephen Decatur Hwy ☎ *800.228.5590* ⏏ *frontiertown.com)* This campground is beautifully situated on the Sinepuxent Bay, so try to reserve your spot early and get a waterfront site. Families who like

doing themed-up vacations will want to stay here because of the Frontier Town Western Theme Park, but there's plenty to do even without that as there is an extra fee to enter the theme park. Talent shows and performances by the local high school choir grace the camp's pavilion. Hayrides, pirate costume contests, treasure hunts in the sand volleyball court and afternoons fishing off the pier are a few of the family pleasures to be had at Frontier Town. That's before you mosey on over to the Western Theme Park (covered elsewhere in this book.) ($)

TREASURE BEACH RV PARK AND CAMPGROUND

(37291 Lighthouse Rd. ☎ *302.436.8001* ⌂ *treasurebeachrvpark.com)* Treasure Beach is great for RV campers who are boating enthusiasts, or those who are looking for a less sandy, blustery experience than Assateague can be. Be sure to check the site map on Treasure Beach's web site when you're making reservations, and try to get a site with a view out onto the open water of the bay. Greater discounts are available for longer stays, and during the summer season a 7-night minimum applies for waterfront sites. The park includes docks and a boat ramp, plus a small skateboard park, recreation center, basketball courts, swimming pool, a crabbing pier, convenience store and Laundromat. ($)

Day Trips

History buffs, shopaholics, and "Wild West" theme park fans will want to plan additional day trips from Ocean City. On the way in or out of town on Route 50, there are two stops to make. The first is for vintage car buffs: **Wheels of Yesterday** *(12708 Ocean Gateway* ☎ *410.213.7329)* is a privately-owned collection of vehicles ranging from a 1928 Lincoln four-door touring car to a 1967 floating Amphicar (its tires act as rudders), from a 1929 Ford Model A fire engine to a couple of vintage family campers. Look up to see their replica Burma-Shave signs, which run down the lengths of the museum's aisles.

The second stop is for ice cream lovers and cheese aficionados. Worcester County's only dairy farm, **Chesapeake Bay Farms** *(2.5 miles west of Berlin on Ocean Gateway* ☎ *410.629.1997* 🖱 *chesapeakebaycheese.com)*, makes ice cream, cheese, and butter using milk from their own dairy cows. There are picnic tables outside for enjoying a cone on the spot, or the staff will pack purchases in ice. A little pen houses the farm's calves outside the shop, convenient for petting and visiting. This may be the most fun your kids have while learning where their food comes from.

ASSATEAGUE ISLAND

Ocean City is a riot of lights and activity, with enough to keep a family busy – or happily idle – for an entire vacation. That said, every Ocean City vacationer should experience Assateague Island at least once, especially since it's so close you can actually see it from Ocean City itself.

Assateague is famous, of course, for its wild horses. Legend has it that the horses survived a Spanish cargo shipwreck off the coast of Virginia, but there is no historical record to confirm this. Another theory is that the horses are descendants of animals brought to the barrier island for grazing in the late 17th century by mainland owners. These sturdy, tough creatures are able to survive the intense heat, scarce food, and stormy weather of Assateague, roaming the island in small herds.

The Maryland herds are kept separate from the Virginia (Chincoteague) herds by a large fence that completely divides the Maryland and Virginia portions of the island. The horses in Virginia can only be viewed from a distance, while the Maryland herds wander around everywhere. Campers sometimes emerge from their tents in the morning to find a few horses milling around the campsite. Though the horses seem tame and accessible, it cannot be emphasized enough that they are not to be touched or fed, for your health and safety and for theirs.

If you don't set foot outside of Ocean City limits for the rest of your stay, you should certainly make the trip to Assateague to see the wild horses and to witness exactly what Ocean City would look like if there were no buildings and no offshore sand replenishment to its beaches. Truly, Assateague is a must-see stop.

ASSATEAGUE ISLAND NATIONAL SEASHORE AND ASSATEAGUE STATE PARK

(Seashore: ☎ *410.641.1441* ⏚ *nps.gov/asis,* **Park:** ☎ *410.641.2120* ⏚ *dnr.state.md.us/publiclands/eastern/assateague.html)* Wind and ocean waves buffet this barrier island, pushing it ever westward and creating a beautifully rugged and ever-changing landscape of sand, marsh grasses and stocky trees. There is both a national seashore and a state park on Assateague, and both have walking/biking trails, beaches, campgrounds, opportunities for paddling, and educational programs including guided boat tours.

Both the state park and the national seashore have useful maps on their web sites. You can always pick up maps and information at the parks themselves, but it is useful to have an idea of the layout before arriving.

Note that pets are prohibited on the Virginia side of the island, and in the state park. They are permitted, leashed, at the national seashore, but not on the trails, in the backcountry campsites, or on the lifeguard-protected beach. Though it might seem like fun to take your dog with you to Assateague, you don't know how the pooch would react to the wild ponies. For these reasons, bringing the dog is probably not such a good idea.

HIKING/BIKING

For a series of three easy family hikes – strolls, really – drive past the state park and into the national seashore. It has three beautifully maintained trails with educational signage.

The *Life of the Marsh* trail is a handicap-accessible boardwalk that loops through a salt marsh on the Sinepuxent Bay. Birdwatchers will enjoy views of the bay and the snowy egrets, marsh hawks and other shore birds commonly seen there.

The *Life of the Forest* trail is another accessible trail that winds through a maritime forest of loblolly pines, sweet gum and oak trees, along with serviceberry and blueberry bushes, and impenetrable thickets of thorny greenbrier and poison ivy. (Don't worry: the trail is well maintained, and if you stay on it as you should, there is little chance of coming into contact with poison ivy.) This is the habitat of nesting owls and woodpeckers, and the eastern towhee, a year-round Assateague resident that spends much of its time foraging for food under fallen leaves.

The *Life of the Dunes* trail is especially interesting because on it there is an artifact of the development that almost took place on the barrier island in the 1950s: a fragment of an old paved road, and a street sign stand on a portion of the trail, creating a strange and incongruous sight in this windswept landscape.

In 1962, a massive storm washed over Assateague, which was then platted with roads and power lines, and a few structures in what was to have been another resort development. The island was completely swamped in most places and all the "improvements" were washed to sea. The project was scrapped and Assateague Island National Seashore was founded when the developers were unable to get permission to build protective seawalls. In fact, Assateague could have been built up just like Ocean City; and, on the other hand, Ocean City could have been like Assateague if not for the development and ongoing protection of the inlet. In any case, the dune trails illustrate how tenacious trees and shrubs get a foothold in the sandy, windy environment and hang on, creating shelter for other plant and animal life. This transitional landscape is rugged and harsh, in startling contrast to the rolling, soft Eastern Shore farmland so nearby.

For a more substantial hike, start walking down the beach itself. If you head south from the guarded beach, you'll be practically on your own after a few hundred yards. The beach is wide and flat, and it just goes on and on, all the way to the Virginia border some 12 miles south. Watch out for vehicles on the beach, as the national seashore does issue permits for over-sand vehicles. See their website for specifics.

CAMPING
Unless you are a hale and hearty camper, plan to camp at Assateague in April or early May, before the mosquitoes and horseflies get really intense, and the sand fleas hatch. If camp in the spring or fall, the intense winds should be your only camping challenge.

Camping is available at both the state park and the national seashore on the Maryland side. The Maryland campground, which is open from April through October, has several bathhouses with hot and cold water, dishwashing stations and nice, clean restrooms. The national seashore side, open all year, is more primitive, with cold showers and chemical toilets. No camping is permitted on the Virginia side of the island.

Reservations are a must at the state park. It is possible to reserve a campsite up to one year in advance. For June, July, and Au-

August camping trips, this is advisable. April and May don't fill up as quickly, but you'll want to make your reservations by about January. The state park's web site is functional but clunky. Their phone reservation operators are friendly and quite knowledgeable about the park. The state park also has a well-stocked camp store and a snack shop.

Reservations for the national seashore campground can be made for April 15 through October 15 and, like the state park, are necessary because slots fill up early. In the off-season, and for backcountry sites, camping is available on a first-come, first-served basis.

Unlike the state park, the national seashore has campsites both beachside and on the shores of the Chincoteague Bay. Again with the mosquitoes: if you camp in the summer, opt for a beachside site to take advantage of the Atlantic breezes (the sand fleas will still be an issue). During the spring and fall, though, the bayside has the advantage of its beautiful sunsets and calmer air. The ocean winds drive away bugs, true, but they can also blow away your tent and kitchen, your chair, and your entire campsite if it is not well secured!

The national seashore also has two ocean-side and four bayside backcountry camping areas that can accommodate up to twenty-five people each. They cannot be reserved in advance. The sites are from 2.5 to 13 miles away from the Maryland ranger station, and can only be reached by hiking or paddling. No freshwater is available, though each site is equipped with a chemical toilet. Bayside sites can be closed during the hunting season, and the ocean sites may be closed due to bird nesting.

If you're thinking of doing a backcountry camping trip at Assateague on a lark, think again. This is not for the inexperienced camper. Backcountry camping must be planned carefully and undertaken not as a whimsical side trip to your Ocean City vacation, but as a thoughtful excursion into the wilderness. Don't go backcountry camping on the bayside in the summertime! Even the National Park Service information discourages this because of the intense bugginess of the salt marshes. For more information, check the **national seashore** web site *(✆ nps.gov/asis)*.

PADDLING

Paddling is, without a doubt, the best way to experience the bayside of Assateague Island. You can rent canoes and kayaks (as well as bicycles) at a stand at the end of Bayside Drive, which is a right turn off of Bayberry Drive if you're headed south, just past the ranger station, **Coastal Bays Program** *(☎ 410.213.BAYS ✆ mdcoastalbays.org)*. From their dock, head south and enjoy the quiet, flat bay views of Assateague without the cars and crowds on the road during the summer season. The wind often picks up a little bit in the afternoon, so morning is ideal for a placid paddling trip.

BOAT TOURS

Several commercial tours of Assateague Island are available by boat. This can be a good way to see the bayside of the island and learn about its history and the ecology. It can also be a good way to overwhelm your vacation budget.

An exception to the expensive prices, **Talbot Street at the Bay** *(☎ 410.289.3500 ✆ talbotstreetpier.com)*, can be found at the Talbot Street Pier right in Ocean City. For $16 ($8 for children 5 to 12) you can board the Assateague Adventure, cruise past Ocean City's commercial fishing pier (interesting in its own right) and loop around the Sinepuxent Bay. The boat even makes a stop on Assateague Island. This is definitely Assateague Lite, as the whole thing only lasts an hour and a half. However, this might be the right level of engagement for a young family or a very quick vacation.

EDUCATIONAL PROGRAMS

The whole Assateague experience is educational. However, if you're looking for structured nature walks, bird-watching tours, and lots of good information about the island, check in at the **Barrier Island Visitors Center** on Route 611, just before the bridge across the Sinepuxent Bay.

To get to Assateague from Ocean City, take Route 50 out of Ocean City, and turn left on Route 611. Route 611 crosses Sinepuxent Bay and ends on Assateague Island. The first right, Bayberry Drive, is the road that extends south to the national seashore. The second right leads to the state park. There is no roadway connecting the Maryland portion of the island with the Virginia section (called the **Chincoteague National Wildlife Refuge**). In fact, there are no roads on a large central section of the island, making it a true wilderness refuge.

FRONTIER TOWN WESTERN THEME PARK

(8428 Stephen Decatur Hwy ☎ *410.641.0057* ☋ *frontiertown.com)* Kids will love this park, and so will any adult with a weakness for cheesy old Western movies. Frontier Town has horse and pony shows, horseback trail rides, a can-can show, and live entertainment all day long. There's a shootout on Main Street every afternoon, and shops and concessions fill this replica of a Wild West town, circa 1860. Check their web site for regularly scheduled Bank Heists, Ceremonial Dances, and Gunfights at the O.K. Corral. Frontier Town also has its own waterpark with water slides, lazy river, giant fun pool and mini golf. To get here from Ocean City, take Route 50 or west to Route 611/Stephen Decatur Highway, and turn left. The park is on the left. Open seasonally.

BERLIN

The small, historic town of Berlin is charming. Even the crankiest husband being dragged on an antiquing expedition must concede this. The town was the location of the movies *Runaway Bride* and

Tuck Everlasting, and it is easy to see why a filmmaker would choose Berlin to represent the bucolic American small town.

The village began in the 1790s, and it is believed its name was a contraction of "Burleigh Inn," a tavern at the crossroads of the town. The town was known as a rest stop for weary travelers in the early days of Ocean City's history. Since the 1980s, Berlin has gone through extensive revamping. Its commercial district and several buildings in town are now listed on the National Register of Historic Places. It is also a Maryland "Main Street Community," designated because of the revitalization efforts.

From Ocean City, take either Route 50 or Route 90 west to Route 113. Go south on 113, and turn right at MD 346, Old Ocean City Boulevard. Follow this to Main Street, in historic Berlin.

Plan to spend an afternoon in Berlin, if not a whole day, to savor the shops, restaurants, and galleries.

THE TAYLOR HOUSE MUSEUM

(208 N Main St. ☎ *410.641.1019* ⌂ *taylorhousemuseum.org)* A gracious restored early 19th century house, the Taylor House Museum is set up to reflect what a well-appointed home would have looked like when it was new, with a gallery in its west wing devoted to local memorabilia. Check the events page on their web site for a fun series of concerts on the lawn, often featuring local and/or traditional music. This is a nice change from many of Ocean City's live music events, which more often than not feature cover bands playing pop or country hits.

TEA BY THE SEA

(7 S Main St. ☎ *410.641.4000)* This utterly authentic, elegant teashop serves its tea in fine bone china and furnishes its tearoom with extremely high-quality antiques. The food served is all made on the premises. Visitors can order afternoon tea, which includes tea sandwiches, scones with clotted cream and spreads, assorted cookies and little cakes, and a pot of tea. Or they can choose full

afternoon tea, which also includes soup and salad. This is definitely the way to go after a late breakfast or brunch, to bridge the gap before dinner. The shop also sells tins of loose teas and tea bags by Harney & Sons and Eastern Shore Tea Company, and organic teas by Davidson's, plus assorted tea accessories.

RAYNE'S REEF LUNCHEONETTE

(10 N Main St. ☎ *410.641.2131)* Rayne's is an old-fashioned sandwich shop with a lunch counter and a menu of traditional sandwiches, burgers, and soda fountain treats. Thursday is half-price burger night, which has become an institution among locals. Service can be spotty, but when at a 50s-style burger joint, somehow that seems okay.

TOWN CENTER ANTIQUES

(1 N Main St. ☎ *410.629.1895)* This sprawling antiques mart is a pleasant place to while away a rainy afternoon. With about 65 dealer stalls in a rambling series of rooms, Town Center Antiques is the place to find furniture of every vintage, old books, hats, jewelry, toys, china, and such random objects as a brass hot water bottle and a ceramic iced tea urn as big as a beach ball. A modest café in the store sells coffee and some baked goods. Open year-round.

A STEP ABOVE GALLERY & GIFTS

(27 N Main St. ⏚ *astepabovegalleryandgifts.com)* This gallery focuses on paintings, sculptures, stained glass, pottery, and "fairy art" made by DelMarVa residents, though there are pieces here from artists farther afield. Their selection of fairy and fantasy art is an unusual touch in this area, which tends to focus on beach-themed art. On the second Friday of every month, A Step Above hosts an art reception as part of Berlin's Second Friday Art Stroll. Open year-round.

BERLIN FARMERS MARKET

(🖱 atbeach.com/farmersmarket) The Berlin Farmers Market bustles with customers and features locally grown food, including organic produce. This market seems to be more bountiful than the one in Ocean City, though the same people organize both. Perhaps it's because Berlin is more of a year-round residential area. Regardless, this market is a great way to support the farmers of the Eastern Shore, and to squeeze some fresh, healthy food into your vacation diet. Open May through November, Wednesdays and Fridays.

THE PINK BOX BAKERY

(120 N Main St. ☎ 410.641.2300 🖱 thepinkboxbakeryandcafe.com) This tiny bakery boasts some interesting regional specialties, including sweet potato biscuits and Smith Island Cake. Declared on October 1, 2008 to be the official dessert of Maryland, Smith Island Cake is a dessert that stands just three inches tall, yet has eight to ten ultra-thin yellow layers, loaded with cooked chocolate fudge icing. The Pink Box Bakery is like a little doll's house, with enough room for just a few customers at a time. Open year-round.

VICTORIAN CHARM

(100 N Main St. ☎ 410.641.6416 🖱 victoriancharm.biz) Vera Bradley's cheerful riot of brightly flowered, quilted handbags, luggage, and fabrics keep this lovely shop from feeling too stuffy and proper. Shoppers will also find Caswell-Massey and Crabtree & Evelyn toiletries, French Provincial table linens, candles, and other French and British-inspired bath and home accessories. Open year-round.

THE GLOBE

(12 Broad St. ☎ 410.641.0784 🖱 globetheater.com) This restaurant and art gallery is housed in the Old Globe Theater, which was built in 1917, condemned in the 1960s, and now carefully restored as a restaurant, gallery space, and small live music venue. Its copper-

topped bar is the warm centerpiece to this sophisticated but friendly restaurant. The fare is a mix of American and Asian-leaning fare, including what they call "The Noodle House," which is a big bowl of noodles served Thai, Cambodian, Vietnamese, or Mongolian style. Thursday night is sushi night at the bar and in the art gallery, with an artful selection of sushi and sashimi, as well as Asian appetizers.

ATLANTIC HOTEL

(2 N Main St. ☎ *410.641.3589* ⊕ *atlantichotel.com)* Built in 1895, this stately hotel sits at the center of downtown Berlin, anchoring the already charming town with its gracious, broad brick porch and manicured landscaping. While there is a modern elevator at the back of the building, the wide wooden staircase at the front door welcomes guests up to the second and third floors, which are bi-sected by very wide hallways with Victorian-era furnishings and enough space to sit and relax. Each floor also has a porch with rocking chairs, for guests who would like a bit more privacy than the front porch provides. All rooms can accommodate two people; deluxe rooms offer a bit more space, but standard rooms are good-sized, too. Each room is furnished with a double bed and authentic Victorian antiques, and baths have either a shower or a claw foot tub. On the first floor of the hotel is the restaurant Solstice.

SOLSTICE /ATLANTIC HOTEL

(2 N Main St. ☎ *410.641.3589* ⊕ *atlantichotel.com)* The Atlantic Hotel has aged gracefully. Solstice, on its first floor, is a stunning re-statement of the Atlantic's classic style. Floors have been stripped and bleached of their dark stain; walls have been coated with sim-ple white and bisque paint. The effect is very sophisticated, yet completely un-fussy and respectful of the hotel's architectural de-tails. Paintings by serious local artists grace the walls, with subjects often including local scenery. The food at Solstice is every bit as sophisticated and elegantly simple as the dining room. The menu

relies on local, seasonal ingredients. Recent selections include Smith Island crab cakes, chicken and dumplings – using gnocchi and truffle broth, no less – and a flatbread pizza with marinated figs, prosciutto, baby rocket and Gorgonzola. Recent desserts include a plum crisp with locally made butter pecan ice cream, bourbon and white chocolate bread pudding, or a simple bowl of blackberries. The brunch menu is equally fabulous. Serious foodies will not want to miss Solstice.

SOLSTICE GENERAL STORE

(17 Jefferson St. ☎ *410.629.0331* ⏁ *atlantichotel.com)* This little shop is the general store for the well-heeled food lover. Those who enjoy packing fancy picnic baskets full of assorted French cheeses, cornichons, organic water crackers, Italian deli sandwiches on artisanal bread, and chilled chardonnay will feel right at home here. Solstice General Store has a gourmet deli, fresh bread, ice cream, kitchen gift items, and other food-related gadgets and fun things. The shop is owned by the Atlantic Hotel, and is tucked just behind it on a side street.

WATER'S EDGE GALLERY

(2 S Main St., 2nd Fl. ☎ *410.629.1784)* Water's Edge is a high-ceilinged, airy gallery space with revolving shows of mostly local art – of which there is plenty. The Eastern Shore provides ample inspiration for landscapes and seascapes, and the Water's Edge does show plenty of high-quality examples of that. Don't expect that to always be the theme, though. One recent show included a modern, abstract series of sculptures made from found objects. To enter, go through the side entrance and up the stairs of the building that houses M.R. Ducks on the ground level.

MERRY SHERWOOD PLANTATION

(8909 Worcester Hwy, Rte 113 ☎ *410.641.2112* ⏁ *merrysherwood.com)* This is a spectacular inn for a romantic getaway. The pre-Civil War

mansion was built in classical Italianate style, looking much like a square cake with a little box on top. The green and white structure has a wide front porch with rockers, and a large fountain in the front garden. The grounds are large and meticulously manicured, with several different flower gardens providing areas to walk, and to sit and visit. Beyond the split-rail fence that marks the back of the property are cornfields. This is fitting, since the mansion was originally part of an extensive plantation, surrounded by fertile fields. The Merry Sherwood is an ideal spot for a girls' weekend away, a honeymoon, or a quiet retreat from the city. The plantation is located on the outskirts of old Berlin, and it feels deliciously isolated from the business of Ocean City.

FURNACE TOWN

If the family has an interest in checking out how very different life was near Ocean City in the early 1800s – or if you're simply sunburned and tired of the beach – Furnace Town and the surrounding area is a great place to spend at least half a day.

FURNACE TOWN LIVING HERITAGE MUSEUM 🔲

(Old Furnace Road at Millville Rd., Snow Hill ☎ *410.632.2032* ☞ *furnacetown.com)* About an hour's drive from Ocean City is an opportunity to take a fascinating look at an early 19th century iron furnace and working village in the Pokomoke Forest. From 1828 to 1850, the Nassawango Iron Furnace and the company that owned it created a "company town" adjacent to a cypress swamp where bog ore was harvested to create pig iron. By 1850, other better types of iron were being made elsewhere and the town was bankrupt. By 1929, only the furnace and some building foundations remained. In the 1960s, restoration of Furnace Town began, and in 1982, the site was opened as a museum complete with costumed interpreters, like Williamsburg.

The towering old furnace in the forest is worth the trip. It is the earliest surviving example of the hot blast process in the nation and is a National Historical Mechanical Engineering Landmark. The kitchen gardens and plantings all around the settlement are carefully labeled, so visitors can get a glimpse of what traditionally grows in the region and their culinary and medicinal uses. The interpreted museum is open seasonally; the grounds are open for walking year-round.

Furnace Town is bordered by a portion of The Nassawango Preserve of The Nature Conservancy. The one-mile walking trail skirts the Nassawango Swamp, crossing it several times with boardwalks. The trail is worth taking, if for no other reason than to get a good look at the swampy forest where bog ore was gathered for the furnace.

From Ocean City, take either Route 50 or Route 90 west to Route 113. Go south on 113 to the town of Snow Hill, and turn right at MD 12/Washington Street/Snow Hill Road. Follow this out of town and turn left at Old Furnace Road.

On your way to or from Furnace Town, make a stop at **Pusey's Country Store** *(5313 Snow Hill Rd.* ☎ *410.632.1992).* This funky general store stocks every good thing from microbrews to mulch. The shop has wood floors and jumbled shelving, and sells a great selection of Maryland wines, Stewarts Sodas, Chincoteague brand soups, and all manner of other local, gourmet, and tasty food. They also sell mulch, plants and other gardening supplies. The store is closed Mondays.

DELAWARE BEACHES

Things change just north of the state line in Delaware. The population density drops, the neon lights fade, and the decibel level lowers. Fenwick Island, and Bethany, Dewey, and Rehoboth Beaches are all an easy drive north on Coastal Highway.

FENWICK ISLAND

Fenwick feels like a quiet northern outpost of Ocean City. The state line is 146th Street, and the shopping and mini-golfing and busyness continues for a few more blocks north into Fenwick Island, Delaware. **The Fenwick Island Lighthouse** *(Lighthouse Road, Fenwick Is. ☎ 302.539.4115 ⌁ fenwickisland.org/ lighthouse.htm)* is a restored light station that dates back to 1859. It's no longer a functioning lighthouse, having been decommissioned in 1978. However, a tenacious group of local residents protested the light being "turned off." In 1981, the Coast Guard turned the property over to the State of Delaware and ultimately returned the original fresnel lens to the lighthouse, which is now symbolically lit.

Fenwick Island Lighthouse is open seasonally, and the view from the top is well worth the climb up the tower's tight spiral staircase. To get to the lighthouse, turn left from Coastal Highway onto 146th Street; the lighthouse is on the right.

BETHANY BEACH

This beautiful, pristine beach community calls itself "The Quiet Resort," and with good reason. Even in the summertime, the sidewalks pretty much roll up after dinner. This is just fine by residents and families who vacation here. Often the most exciting event on a summer afternoon is a game of croquet on one of the wide, grassy spaces in the center of town.

Bethany Beach has a tiny, tidy downtown business district, but for dining and shopping, there are more and better options further north in Rehoboth. Bethany's carefully maintained streets of grand seaside "cottages" are beautiful and moneyed. During the summer months, the town hosts weekend concerts at the bandstand downtown, and celebrates Independence Day with a parade and fireworks on the beach.

Founded at the turn of the 20th century by the religious group Disciples of Christ, Bethany Beach was initially envisioned not as a town but simply as a seaside retreat for Christian groups.

A tabernacle building was constructed, but it leaked terribly. Plus the area's drinking water was poor, a promised train line was not delivered, and the original officers of the Bethany Beach Improvement Company were sacked. It was only after six Pittsburgh businessmen were brought in to get things organized that the town began to take its current shape.

As recently as the 1970s, no alcohol was served in Bethany Beach. While the town is no longer a religious retreat, its roots as an oasis and a place for quiet reflection are still quite evident.

Of all the area seaside resorts, Bethany presents the most vivid contrast to the chock-a-block, rowdy Ocean City. It's fun to wander through Bethany and note the difference between it and its noisy neighbor to the south.

DEWEY BEACH

Washingtonian Magazine labeled Dewey Beach as "Spring Break for Adults." Dewey has a longstanding reputation as the party beach for young professionals from D.C., Baltimore, and Philadelphia. Its year-round population is only about 300, but on summer weekends the crowds can exceed 30,000, with bar-hopping pedestrians clogging Coastal Highway and causing huge traffic jams.

The Bottle & Cork *(1807 Highway One* ☎ *302.227.7272* ✆ *deweybeachlife.com/ent_bc.html)* and **The Rusty Rudder** *(113 Dickinson St.* ☎ *302.227.3888* ✆ *deweybeachlife.com/nl_rr.html)* are two of the most popular bars and venues for live music. **The Starboard** *(2009 Highway One* ☎ *302.227.4600* ✆ *thestarboard.com)* offers make-your-own Bloody Marys at their Suicide Brunch on Sunday mornings.

Dewey Beach tries to bill itself as a family-friendly destination, but the party vibe runs deep. For decades, singles leading buttoned-down professional lives all week have considered this small beach town to be their oasis, renting group houses for the summer and trekking to the beach every weekend. Those who prefer to stay away from the wild party can easily do so: Dewey is just one mile long and two blocks wide.

REHOBOTH BEACH

The most sophisticated of the Delaware beach resorts, Rehoboth Beach has excellent dining and shopping, a small but charming boardwalk, beautiful residential neighborhoods, and nightlife that's fun but not out of control.

Rehoboth also has a large and affluent gay community. Perhaps this is the demographic that has driven the **Rehoboth Beach Theater of the Arts** *(20 Baltimore Ave.* ☎ *301.277.9310* ⊕ *rehoboth-beachtheater.com)* to stage such quirky offerings as "Nice Jewish Girls Gone Bad," "Broadway Fever," "Abbamania", and even "The Vagina Monologues."

If you go to Rehoboth, arrive hungry and stay long enough to eat a few times. Restaurants spring up constantly and the offerings keep getting better and more adventurous. The best source for information on downtown Rehoboth restaurants (as well as shopping and other activities) is definitely the web site maintained by **Rehoboth Beach Main Street, Inc.** *(⊕ rehomain.com)*. Or just wander along Rehoboth Avenue, downtown's main street, or any of several side streets off of it, and peruse the menus posted outside the many restaurant doors.

There are two places worth recommending simply because they're unusual. To scratch that fried beach food itch, skip the traditional Boardwalk fare, which you can get at Ocean City's Boardwalk. Instead, try **go fish!** *(24 Rehoboth Ave.* ☎ *302.226.1044* ⊕ *gofishdelaware.com)*, a tiny fish and chips shop that is gleefully British, with the Union Jack plastered across its sign and a British accent issuing from every staff member. Service is quick, and the fish and chips are fresh and very crisp.

To quench your thirst, do not miss **Dogfish Head Brewings & Eats** *(320 Rehoboth Ave.* ☎ *302.226.2739* ⊕ *dogfish.com)*. This award-winning brewery creates beers with names like Raison D'Atre and Lawnmower. All their beers are made on-site and at a larger brewery a few miles away in Milton, Delaware. Dogfish Head Ale is distributed fairly widely, so look for it back home too. Dogfish Head distills their own spirits as well. Try one of their vodka infusions (chocolate is a perennial favorite).

Shopping in downtown Rehoboth Beach is also a treat, especially if your mind is growing numb from the repetitive, schlocky offerings in most Ocean City shops. Campy and beachy home décor, good quality casual and resort clothing, specialty food and wine, and fine art are to be had at over 200 shops, boutiques, and galleries.

Downtown Rehoboth has three bookstores. **Browseabout Books** *(133 Rehoboth Ave.* ☎ *302.226.2665* ⌐ *browseaboutbooks.com)* is an independent bookstore that hosts local author signings and hosts a book club. **Lambda Rising** *(39 Baltimore Ave.* ☎ *302.227.6969* ⌐ *lambdarising.com),* the gay bookstore that has been a D.C. institution since 1974, also has a Rehoboth Beach location. **Atlantic Books** *(47 Rehoboth Ave.* ☎ *301.227.0490* ⌐ *atlanticbooks.us)* has a location here as well.

The real story about Rehoboth Beach shopping happens west of downtown. Out on Route 1 (Coastal Highway becomes Highway 1 and Route 1, but it's all the same road), a giant **Tanger Outlet** mega-plex, with 130 outlet stores in three separate shopping centers, spans both sides of the road. Bargains can be had at outlet stores for Bose, Coach, J. Crew, Nautica, Waterford Wedgwood, Black & Decker, Disney, Abercrombie & Fitch, Hollister, Lenox, Izod, Bass, Rockport, and on and on. Plus, Delaware has no sales tax, so you'll save a little bit more.

Outlet shopping has lost some of its luster with the proliferation of more outlet centers than can possibly be stocked with factory seconds. Nevertheless, the huge variety and reliable, if not spectacular, discounts make Rehoboth's sprawling Tanger Outlets a key destination for any shopaholic.

Index

D

Days Inn Oceanfront, 116
Delmarva Bike Week, 33
Dewey Beach, 142
disability access, 27
Dog Playground, 27
dogs, bringing, 27
Dolle's Candyland, 43
Donald's Duck Shoppe, 74
Dorchester Beach Volleyball
    Park, 67
Downtown Recreation Complex,
    68
Duffy's Tavern, 90
Dumser's Dairyland, 86
Dumser's Dairyland, 42
Dunes Manor, 117

E

Edge at Fager's Island, 117
Edwards Department Store, 40
Empress Motel, The, 118

F

Fager's Island, 104
Fager's Island Fine Dining, 96
Farmer's Market, Ocean City, 77
Fat Daddy's, 87
Fausto's Antipasti, 97
Fenwick Inn, 122
Fenwick Island, 141
fire of 1925, 18
Fireman's Association
    Conference, 32
Fish Tales, 90
Fisher's Popcorn, 42
Fishing Pier (9th Street), 69

fishing, charter, 47
fishing, pier and surf, 48
Flamingo Motel, The, 118
Flashback Old-Time Photos, 40
Food Lion, 76
Fort Whaley Campground, 125
Fractured Prune, 83
Francis Scott Key Family Resort,
    124
Fresco's Fine Dining, 98
Frontier Town Family
    Campground, 125
Frontier Town Western Theme
    Park, 133
Furnace Town, 139

G

Galaxy 66, 98
General's Kitchen, The, 84
Glen Riddle Golf Club, 64
Globe, The, 136
Gold Down Under, 57
Golf Getaway, Ocean City, 61
Greyhound Bus, 24
Grove Market, 91

H

H2O, 107
Hacienda, La, 92
Hallmark News Center, 73
Hampton House, 112
Happy Jack's Pancake House, 84
Harbour Island Marina, 48
Harrison Hall, 112
Harrison's Harbor Watch, 98
Hilton Suites Ocean City
    Oceanfront, 119
Hobbit, The, 99

ABOUT THE AUTHOR

Kim Kash is a freelance writer based in the Washington, D.C. area, where she writes about food, health, and the environment. She is particularly interested in the local foods movement, and is the co-founder of the Greenbelt Farmers Market. She was born and raised in Greenbelt, Maryland, and lived for several years in California. Living on the west coast gave her a deeper appreciation for the seasons and the weathered charm of the mid-Atlantic states.

NOTES:

NOTES:

NOTES:

TOURIST TOWN GUIDES™

Explore America's
Fun Places

Books in the *Tourist Town Guides*™ series are available at bookstores and online. You can also visit our website for additional book and travel information. The address is:

http://www.touristtown.com

www.touristtown.com

ORDER FORM #1
ON REVERSE SIDE

Tourist Town Guides™ is published by:

Channel Lake, Inc.
P.O. Box 1771
New York, NY 10156

TOURIST TOWN GUIDES™
ORDER FORM

Telephone: With your credit card handy,
call toll-free 800.592.1566

Fax: Send this form toll-free to 866.794.5507

E-mail: Send the information on this form
to orders@channellake.com

Postal mail: Send this form with payment to Channel Lake, Inc.
P.O. Box 1771, New York, NY, 10156

Your Information: ( ) Do not add me to your mailing list

Name: _____

Address: _____

City: _____ State: _____ Zip: _____

Telephone: _____

E-mail: _____

Book Title(s) / ISBN(s) / Quantity / Price
(see previous pages or www.touristtown.com for this information)

_____

_____

_____

Total payment*: $_____

Payment Information: (Circle One)   Visa / Mastercard

Number: _____ Exp: _____

Or, make check payable to: **Channel Lake, Inc.**

* Add the lesser of $6.50 USD or 18% of the total purchase price for shipping. International orders call or e-mail first! New York orders add 8% sales tax.

**ORDER FORM #2
ON REVERSE SIDE**

(for additional orders)

Tourist Town Guides™ is published by:

Channel Lake, Inc.
P.O. Box 1771
New York, NY 10156

TOURIST TOWN GUIDES™
ORDER FORM

Telephone: With your credit card handy,
call toll-free 800.592.1566

Fax: Send this form toll-free to 866.794.5507

E-mail: Send the information on this form
to orders@channellake.com

Postal mail: Send this form with payment to Channel Lake, Inc.
P.O. Box 1771, New York, NY, 10156

Your Information: ( ) Do not add me to your mailing list

Name: _____

Address: _____

City: _____ State: _____ Zip: _____

Telephone: _____

E-mail: _____

Book Title(s) / ISBN(s) / Quantity / Price
(see previous pages or www.touristtown.com for this information)

_____

_____

_____

Total payment*: $_____

Payment Information: (Circle One)   Visa / Mastercard

Number: _____ Exp: _____

Or, make check payable to: **Channel Lake, Inc.**

* Add the lesser of $6.50 USD or 18% of the total purchase price for shipping. International orders call or e-mail first! New York orders add 8% sales tax.